ALSO BY SCOTT RITTER

Endgame
War on Iraq
Frontier Justice
Iraq Confidential
Target Iran

WAGING PEACE

WAGING PEACE

The Art of War for the Antiwar Movement

SCOTT RITTER

Nation Books
New York
www.nationbooks.org

WAGING PEACE:
The Art of War for the Antiwar Movement

Published by Nation Books
An Imprint of Avalon Publishing Group, Inc.
245 West 17th Street, 11th Floor
New York, NY 10011

Nation Books is a copublishing venture of the Nation Institute and Avalon Publishing Group, Incorporated.

Library of Congress Cataloging-in-Publication Data is available.

ISBN-13: 978-1-56858-328-0
ISBN-10: 1-56858-328-1

9 8 7 6 5 4 3 2 1

Book design by Bettina Wilhelm
Printed in the United States of America
Distributed by Publishers Group West

CONTENTS

Acknowledgments VII

Introduction: Life as Conflict XI

1 On Losing 1

2 Waging Peace 15

3 The Art of War 27

4 Decision Making 41

5 Intelligence Preparation of the Battlefield 51

6 Strategy, Operations, Tactics and the Art of Campaigning 59

7 Organization and Incident Command 73

Conclusion: On Winning 87

Intelligence Preparation of the Battlefield (IPB) Support Graphic Template (Notional Demonstration Activity) 101

Decision Making: The "OODA-Loop" 103

Appendix A: The Constitution of the United States of America 105

Appendix B: The Charter of the United Nations 133

Index 169

Acknowledgments

If I had my way, this book would never have been written. To be honest, the book I want to write (and have been working on now for several years) concerns the history of Soviet Central Asia, not a critique of the antiwar movement. But events have a way of intervening. My most recent efforts to write my history book were disrupted on the morning of July 7, 2005, as I was making my way to the British Archives in London. I was less than three hundred yards from where a terrorist bomber blew apart a London commuter bus, killing and injuring dozens as part of a larger terror attack that day. I joined thousands of others in fleeing the area, and in doing so placed my personal research and writing project on hold.

The war on terror is something we all wish wasn't a reality. In the same way, we all wish that the circumstances in the Middle East were such that America was not involved in an ongoing conflict in Iraq, or preparing for another conflict with Iran. These conflicts, or threats thereof, are as real as the terrorist bombs that ripped apart London in July 2005, or the hijacked airliners that brought down the World Trade Center and part of the Pentagon in September 2001. They are real, and I, like many others, have found myself thrown into the mix. These circumstances have led to this book.

This is a book written in the spirit of friendship. It is a by-product of countless hours of joint work between myself and my fellow practitioners of peace and justice across the United States and around the world. There well may be those who read this book and question my choice of words and emphasis. But let no one question my heart, which has been uplifted by the hard work of so many individuals and organizations dedicated to waging peace. From Bethlehem Neighbors for Peace right here in my hometown of Delmar, New York; to the wonderful women of Code Pink and their intrepid leader, Medea Benjamin; to the Burlington, Vermont, Peace and Justice Center; to those who support the cause of peace from Paducah, Kentucky, to West Palm Beach, Florida; I have been honored with the opportunity to experience the passion and commitment they all bring to what basically boils down to "doing the right thing."

While I cannot possibly list everyone with whom I have had the privilege of working over these past years (and I beg the forgiveness of any who feel slighted should I have failed to make mention of you or your groups), I would be remiss not to point out those with whom I feel I have been engaged in an endless journey toward a world where war is not seen as the solution to all that ails us. To Sunny Miller and Charles Jenks at the Traprock Peace Center, I owe much not only in terms of helping get the word out in New England and elsewhere but also because they have stuck by me through thick and thin, when the easy course of action would have been to walk away. The same can be said of Alan Chartock and the staff of WAMC radio in Albany, New York.

To Robin Ennis-Cantwell and everyone in Seattle, to the hundreds of people in Los Angeles, San Francisco, and all points in between, thanks for making my numerous visits to the West Coast the pleasant experiences they always were. I would also like to thank Jeff Norman and U.S. Tour of Duty for helping get not only my voice heard but also the voices of all those who otherwise would have been ignored by the mainstream media. To Bill and Cindy Cole, I thank you for your friendship and for making Chester, Vermont, seem like a home away from home for me and my family. And a special mention goes out to Mary Lou Cook in Santa Fe, New Mexico, who was one of the first who tried to turn this practitioner of war into a practitioner of peace.

I would like to thank a very special woman, Betty Williams, and her fantastic associate, Rusti Findlay, for allowing me into their lives and their work. To have the opportunity to interact with a Nobel Peace laureate is a very special treat. To work with one as gifted as Betty, and to have the opportunity to meet other women Nobel Peace laureates, is a truly unique opportunity for which I am forever grateful.

A book doesn't get written without an editor and a publisher. The relationship I have developed over the past years with Nation Books, the Nation Institute, and Avalon Publishing Group has been nothing short of spectacular (at least from my perspective). To Carl Bromley, thank you for having the vision to see a book where once there was just an idea. To Hamilton Fish and Katrina vanden Heuvel, thank you for your ongoing support, and for making this "conservative Republican" feel right at home among the *Nation* family. And for Anne Sullivan at Avalon, no one could ask for a better interface with the media. Your friendship and professionalism are greatly appreciated.

While this is a book about waging peace, I must note that I found motivation for writing it not only among the wonderful people who comprise the peace and justice movement as a whole but also among my friends and colleagues in the fire service across America. Some may find an inherent lack of association between "peaceniks" and firefighters. I do not. The value systems in play among both groups are very much the same, and if there is any hope of bringing mainstream America into the cause of peace and justice, there needs to be better interaction between not only these two communities but also all communities that comprise the United States of America. So I thank and salute my fellow firefighters of the Delmar Fire Department, all the fire departments that comprise the town of Bethlehem, and my friends and colleagues at Poughkeepsie Fire Department Station 2; the Houston HAZMAT Incident Response Team; the Burlington (Vermont) firefighters; Mount Vernon, New York; and all others who have provided friendship and support, and who serve their country and communities with such pride and professionalism.

Last but not least are my family and friends, without whom nothing would be worth doing. To Bob and Amy Murphy, their son Ryan, and all the others who comprise my Albany circle of friends, I thank you for everything you've done for me and my family over the years. To Chris Cobb-Smith, Roger Hill, and John Sartorious, your friendship and support will always be remembered, and hopefully returned in full. To my parents, Bill and Pat Ritter, and my sisters Shirley, Suzanne, and Amy, and their respective families, and to my cousins Jenny and Sam, and my Aunt Shirley and Uncle Tom, thanks for everything. And, of course, to my loving wife, Marina, my two wonderful daughters, Patty and Vicka, and a most supportive father-in-law, Bidzina, there would be nothing worth doing without your love and support. Hopefully there is some way this book can help pave the way for a better world for us all.

Scott Ritter
Delmar, New York
January 2007

Introduction

LIFE AS CONFLICT

Peace is not the absence of conflict but the presence of creative alternatives for responding to conflict—alternatives to passive or aggressive responses, alternatives to violence.

—*Dorothy Thompson*

* * *

This book is not for everyone. There will be those among the antiwar movement who will, out of some misguided sense of principle, be repulsed by the notion of their movement embracing something as noxious as the Art of War. And then there are those who are disdainful of the antiwar movement who will question why I, a former officer of Marines, would want to write a book that seeks to better organize a social movement that they see as being diametrically opposed to everything I and the Marine Corps I proudly served. Let me make it quite easy for those who fall into either camp, or for that matter, for anyone who approaches this book with anything other than an open mind. This book is not for you. Quit reading, close the cover, and move on.

If you are still reading this, then I either haven't quite convinced you that you are wasting your time, or you are inquisitive enough to realize that there might be something in this slim volume that could pertain to you. Read on.

I have no way of knowing exactly what category of person you are, except to say that, broadly speaking, you fall into one of three camps: the Warrior, the Observer, or the Pacifist. Each term in and of itself is a gross generalization, but in short you are either someone who confronts a problem head-on, someone who takes a neutral position when confronted by a problem, or someone who simply wishes the problem would go away.

Conventional wisdom would hold that flag-waving pro-soldier Americans would naturally fall into the Warrior category, that hand-wringing antiwar activists would fall into the 'Pacifist' category, and most mainstream Americans would fall into the Observer category. This is patently wrong.

Depending on any given issue, people can morph into any one of these three categories, or a variation thereof. An antiwar activist who aggressively pursues a counter-recruitment campaign can be very much a Warrior, while a retired military officer who proudly supports the troops overseas can become quite the Pacifist when confronted by social injustice. And we all have been simple Observers more times than we like to admit.

I start out with the premise that life is conflict, given that I define conflict as the existence of friction created when two or more forces interact. In this regard, the mere act of waking up in the morning is in fact conflict, given that you are interacting with the forces of gravity as you rise from bed, creating a dynamic of resistance and counter-resistance, which causes friction, consuming energy and beginning the process of tiring as soon as you have risen from your rest. Conflict is constant, and ongoing. Conflict is life. We simply don't realize this as we get on with our daily routines because we have already factored in conflict, and our responses to it, as part of the norm that defines our life.

Not all conflict is violent. In fact, most of the conflicts we encounter on a daily basis are nonconfrontational in nature, simply because we have derived strategies, operations, and tactics to deal with them. We just don't call it that. Our body is in a constant state of conflict, consuming energy, which needs to be replenished if we are to survive. We need to preserve body temperature, so we clothe ourselves. We need to nourish ourselves, so we procure food and eat. We need to protect ourselves from disease, so we bathe and provide for basic sanitation. We fight the elements, hunger, and germs—a constant, ongoing series of conflicts.

Yet we deal with it, almost without thinking. For instance, we need food, so we go to the store. But it isn't that simple. There are a whole host of factors at play. We deal with time/distance factors by using a car. We need to factor in putting gas in the car, seeking the best route to the store, navigation issues, parking, choosing which food to buy, allocating money for the purchases, storing the food at home, and preparing the food. If one parses all of the elements at play in the simple act of acquiring food, you will see that there are innumerable points of friction occurring, conflict after conflict, each of which requires a systematic approach in order to be overcome, individually and collectively. This systematic approach is, in essence, the Art of War, executed on a daily basis by every man, woman, and child. We just don't call it that, and don't think of it in those terms.

Life is conflict. Accept this, and you're on the path toward dealing effectively with this conflict. Pretend that conflict doesn't exist, and you will be defeated, over and over again, as the reality of our conflict-dominated world consumes you. Conflict resolution doesn't have to be violent. Indeed, a key element of the Art of War is to find alternatives to violence to resolve conflict situations. Violence generates the greatest amount of friction possible. The ideal conflict resolution situation is one that produces the least amount of friction. The smoother a process operates the better functioning it is.

Life is a process of inherent friction. Our goal in creating the opportunities for success is to find the way to reduce friction in a systematic, manageable fashion. We do this on a daily basis in our personal lives. And the military does this as well, on a different scale, using strategies and tactics that have been defined in a martial sense, but which are directly applicable, and indeed paralleled, in our own daily existence. In order for the antiwar movement, or any movement or organization for that matter, to succeed, it will need to accept the reality that it is engaged in ongoing conflict, or "war"—not only with its ideological opponents but also within its own organization—and then adopt the appropriate methodologies of action and organizational structure to best deal with these conflicts. This is the Art of War.

What is clear is that most of us practice the Art of War every day. Most of us are Warriors when it comes to dealing with the conflicts we face on a constant basis, such as feeding ourselves. Warriors eat. Observers go hungry. And Pacifists starve. The key is capturing the Warrior mentality and organizing it so that all of life's conflicts can be resolved with the same efficiency that most of us bring to bear on the relatively simple matter of feeding ourselves and our family. This is the Art of War applied.

If you're still reading this, and find yourself attracted by the basic concept put forward here, then this book is for you, whether you are Antiwar, pro–Peace and Justice, or simply a schoolteacher, business professional, or homemaker interested in alternative means of dealing with and resolving conflict. Read on, learn, and enjoy.

1

On Losing

If you can accept losing you can't win.
—Vince Lombardi

* * *

Having accepted that life is conflict, we need to *study* closely the above quote by legendary football coach Vince Lombardi. If life is conflict, and you lose, you die. So, if one learns to accept losing, it is not that you simply can't win, you can't survive. This is a hard truth in times of war, when losing on the field of battle often means death. But as I said in the introduction, not all conflict in life is violent. "Survival" does not automatically equate to life over death. If one accepts the Webster's dictionary definition of survival as "a natural process resulting in the evolution of organisms best adapted to the environment," losing means that another system or force has evolved in a manner that is better adapted to a given environment than you are. It means you are subordinate. It means your will has been suppressed.

My working assumption in writing this book is that the antiwar movement in America is losing its struggle in the name of peace and justice. This is a hard critique, one that doesn't go over well within an organization composed of so many well-meaning individuals who have made great sacrifices in support of their cause. But it is an accurate one nonetheless.

The genesis of this book lies in an article I wrote, "The Art of War for the Antiwar Movement," published April 1, 2006, on AlterNet (see www.AlterNet.org). In order to best establish the foundation for this book, I offer the article here in its entirety:

> In the months leading up to the invasion of Iraq by a U.S.-led coalition, and for three years since, I have spent many hours speaking to numerous antiwar forums across the country and around the world. I have always been struck by the sincerity of the vast majority of those who call themselves antiwar, and have been impressed by their willingness to give so much of themselves in the service of such a noble cause.
>
> Whether participating in demonstrations, organizing a vigil, conducting town-hall meetings, or writing letters to their elected officials and the media, the participants in the antiwar movement have exhibited an energy and integrity that would make anyone proud. For myself, I have been vociferous in my defense of the actions of the majority of the antiwar movement, noting that the expression of their views is not only consistent with their rights afforded by the Constitution of the United States, but also that their engagement in the process of citizenship is a stellar example of the ideals and values set forth in that document, and as such representative of the highest form of patriotism in keeping with service to a document that begins, "We the People."
>
> Lately I have noticed a growing despondency among many of those who call themselves the antiwar movement. With the United States now entering its fourth year of

illegal war in and illegitimate occupation of Iraq, and the pro-war movement moving inexorably toward yet another disastrous conflict with Iran, there is an increasing awareness that the cause of the antiwar movement, no matter how noble and worthy, is in fact a losing cause as currently executed. Despite all of the well-meaning and patriotic work of the millions of activists and citizens who comprise the antiwar movement, America still remains very much a nation engaged in waging and planning wars of aggression and has become a nation that increasingly identifies itself through its military and the wars it fights. This is a sad manifestation of the fact that the American people seem to be addicted to war and violence, rather than the ideals of human rights, individual liberty, and freedom and justice for all that should define our nation.

In short, the antiwar movement has come face-to-face with the reality that in the ongoing war of ideologies that is being waged in America today, their cause is not just losing, but is in fact on the verge of complete collapse. Many in the antiwar movement would take exception to such a characterization of the situation, given the fact that there seems to be a growing change in the mood among Americans against the ongoing war in Iraq. But one only has to scratch at the surface of this public discontent to realize how shallow and superficial it is. Americans aren't against the war in Iraq because it is wrong; they are against it because we are losing.

Take the example of Congressman Jack Murtha. A vocal supporter of President Bush's decision to invade Iraq, in the fall of 2005 Mr. Murtha went public with his dramatic change of position, suddenly rejecting the war as unwinnable and demanding the immediate withdrawal of

American troops from Iraq. While his standards were laudable, I have serious problems with Jack Murtha's thought process here. At what point did the American invasion of Iraq become a bad war? When we suffered 2,000 dead? After two years of fruitless struggle? Once we spent $100 billion?

While vocalizing his current opposition against the Iraq War, Congressman Murtha and others who voted for the war but now question its merits have never retracted their original pro-war stance. Nor have they criticized their role in abrogating the Constitutional processes for bringing our country into conflict when they voted for a war before the President had publicly committed to going to war (we now know the President had committed to the invasion of Iraq by the summer of 2002, and that all his representations to the American people and Congress about "war as a matter of last resort" and "seeking a diplomatic solution" were bald-faced lies). The Iraq War was wrong the moment we started bombing Iraq. Getting rid of Saddam Hussein is no excuse, and does not pardon America's collective sin of brooking and tolerating an illegal war of aggression.

The reality is, had our military prevailed in this struggle, the American people for the most part would not even blink at the moral and legal arguments against this war. This underlying reality is reflected in the fact that despite our ongoing disaster in Iraq, America is propelled down a course of action that leads us toward conflict with Iran. President Bush recently reaffirmed his embrace of the principles of preemptive war when he signed off on the 2006 version of the National Security Strategy of the United States, which highlights Iran as a threat worthy of confrontation. This event has gone virtually unmentioned by the American mainstream media, unremarked by a Congress that remains complicit in the war-mongering policies of the Bush administration, and unnoticed by the majority of Americans. America is preprogrammed for war, and unless the antiwar movement dramatically changes the manner in which it conducts its struggle, America will become a nation of war, for war, and defined by war, and as such a nation that will ultimately be consumed by war.

It is high time for the antiwar movement to take a collective look in the mirror, and be honest about what they see: a poorly organized, chaotic, and indeed often anarchic conglomeration of egos, pet projects, and idealism that barely constitutes a "movement," let alone a winning cause. I have yet to observe an antiwar demonstration that has a focus on antiwar. It often seemed that every left-wing cause took advantage of the event to promote its own particular agenda, so that "No War in Iraq" shared the stage with the environment, ecology, animal rights, pro-choice, and numerous other causes that not only diluted the antiwar message that was supposed to be sent, but also guaranteed that the demonstration itself would be seen as something hijacked by the left, inclusive of only progressive ideologues, and exclusive of the vast majority of moderate (and even conservative) Americans who might have wanted to share the stage with their fellow Americans from the left when it comes to opposing war with Iraq (or even Iran), but do not want to be associated with any other theme.

The antiwar movement, first and foremost, needs to develop a laser-like focus on being nothing more or less than antiwar.

The antiwar movement lacks any notion of strategic thinking, operational planning, or sense of sound tactics. So much energy is wasted because of this failure to centrally plan and organize. As a result, when the antiwar movement does get it right (and on occasion it does), the success is frittered away by a failure to have planned effective follow-up efforts, failure to have implemented any supporting operations, an inability to recognize opportunities as they emerge, and a lack of resources to exploit such opportunities if in fact they were recognized to begin with. In short, the antiwar movement is little more than a walk-on squad of high school football players who draw plays in the sand, taking on the National Football League Super Bowl Champions.

In order to even have a chance of prevailing with the American people, the antiwar movement is going to need much more than just good ideals and values. It needs to start thinking like a warrior would, in full recognition that we as a nation are engaged in a life-or-death struggle of competing ideologies with those who promote war as an American value and virtue.

The antiwar movement needs to study the philosophies of those who have mastered the art of conflict, from Caesar to Napoleon, from Sun Tzu to Clausewitz. It needs to study the "enemy," learning to understand the pro-war movement as well as it understands itself. It needs to comprehend the art of campaigning, of waging battles only when necessary, and having the ability to wage a struggle on several fronts simultaneously, synchronizing each struggle so that a synergy is created that maximizes whatever energy is being expended. The antiwar movement needs to understand the pro-war movement's center of gravity, and design measures to defeat this. It needs to grasp the pro-war movement's decision-making cycle, then undertake a comprehensive course of action that learns to preempt this cycle, getting "inside" the pro-war system of making decisions, and thereby forcing the pro-war movement to react to the antiwar agenda, instead of vice versa.

There is an old adage in the military that "intelligence drives operations." The antiwar movement needs to develop a centralized intelligence operation—not a spy organization, but rather a think tank that produces sound analysis based upon facts that can be used to empower those who are waging the struggle against war. Far too often the antiwar movement dilutes its effectiveness by either being unable to produce facts during a debate, or when it does, producing facts that are inaccurate, incomplete, or both. The mainstream media treats the antiwar movement as a joke because many times that is exactly what the antiwar movement, through its lack of preparation and grasp of the facts, allows itself to become.

The antiwar movement lacks organization. There is no central leadership, or mechanism to effectively muster and control resources. The antiwar movement takes pride in its "democratic" composition, but in fact it operates as little more than controlled chaos, creating ample opportunity for the pro-war movement to effectively execute a divide-and-conquer strategy to minimize and nullify whatever good the antiwar movement achieves through its efforts. The antiwar movement would do well to take a page from the fire service and implement a version of the Incident Command System (ICS) that firefighters use when fighting complex fires involving the integration of several departments, organizations, and jurisdictions. The antiwar movement needs to develop its own "ICS for the antiwar" that is universally applied throughout the movement, so that an antiwar effort in Seattle, Washington, operates the same as an antiwar effort in New York City, and as such can be coordinated and controlled by an overall command staff operating from Denver, Colorado.

Complex problems, such as those faced by the antiwar movement, require complex solutions, which in turn dictate a flexible control mechanism that can coordinate and synchronize every effort to achieve the desired result at a time and place of the antiwar movement's choosing, and then be prepared to follow up on successes as they occur and sustain the movement over an extended period of time. It is not enough to win a battle against the pro-war movement; the antiwar movement needs to win the war of ideologies. As such it must prepare not only to win a particular fight but also to exploit that victory, massing its forces against any developed weakness, and drive the pro-war movement into the ground and off the American political map once and for all.

I have indicated my willingness to apply my training and experience as a warrior in a manner that helps teach the principles of the Art of War to those who call themselves part of the antiwar movement. There seems to be not only a need for this sort of training but also a desire among the myriad of individuals and groups who comprise the antiwar movement for an overall coordinated strategic direction, operational planning, and tactical execution of agreed-upon mission objectives. One can be certain that the pro-war movement is conducting itself in full accordance with these very same organizational principles and methodologies. And let there be no doubt: the pro-war movement in America is prevailing. In order to gain the upper hand politically, and actually position itself to stop those wars already being fought (Iraq) and prevent those being planned (Iran), the antiwar movement will need to

> reexamine in totality the way it does business. I for one am ready to assist. However, in writing this essay, I am constantly reminded of the old saying, "You can lead a horse to water, but you can't make it drink." One can only hope that the antiwar movement is thirsty.

In reviewing the many comments that appeared on the AlterNet blog following the posting of this article, it was clear to me that many people out there "got it." It was also clear to me that there were many others who did not. Among those who took exception to my article were two local activists from New York with whom I had interacted in the past. On April 19, 2006, these activists, Maureen Aumand and Steve Breyman, published an article on the Common Dreams Web site (www.CommonDreams.org), *Ritter Gets it Wrong: Why All the Negativity?*

Aumand and Breyman came out swinging. "It's odd," they wrote, "that just as the tide turns irrevocably against the U.S. occupation of Iraq—both here and there—the otherwise steady Scott Ritter panics." Apparently in my panicked state of mind I had failed to see that the antiwar movement (which the two activists prefer to call the "peace movement") was, in fact, winning. Again, Aumand and Breyman:

> For some indicators of the health of the peace movement, let's take a look at just the last half-year or so. The AFL-CIO called for the "rapid return" of troops in Iraq in July 2005. Dozens of local, state, and national labor organizations passed similar, often stronger resolutions. Some one hundred or more municipalities across the country—including Baltimore, Chicago, Philadelphia, and San Francisco—passed resolutions to bring the troops home. Public opinion turned strongly against the

war—and the war president—as shown by a torrent of polls. The opinions of the troops in Iraq were polled recently: 72 percent were for complete withdrawal by the end of 2006. Faith communities weighed in. The Union of Reform Judaism—the spiritual home of a million and a half American Jews—resolved last November to bring the troops home. The United Methodist Church—whose members include George Bush and Dick Cheney—called not only for troop withdrawal in October 2005, but for accountability for those "responsible for leading us into this disastrous war." Thousands of former military personnel (including Gen. Newbold most recently), diplomats, and intelligence professionals denounced the war and actively oppose it.

Several new antiwar veterans' organizations—led by those who served and bled in Iraq—have formed. Coordinated citizen lobbying efforts have changed and emboldened members of Congress leading to a growing menu of antiwar bills. "Full disclosure" military recruitment campaigns continue to bedevil army recruiters, who are finding it harder to sign up enough youth to keep the war going. Thousands of antiwar events took place across the country on the war's third anniversary. The agitation for a Department of Peace gathers steam in the midst of Bush's failed preemptive war. Increasingly coordinated and focused political efforts challenge congressional incumbents whose cowardice and failure in the face of the will to war permits the debacle to proceed. We're currently gearing up for the season's big antiwar demonstration in New York City on April 29. This does not sound to us like a "losing cause" or a movement on the "verge of complete collapse."

As I write this, America is soaking in the reality of the true meaning of the Democratic Party's electoral achievement in winning back the Senate and the House of Representatives. The war in Iraq still rages. From all accounts, the prevailing opinion in Washington, D.C., has tens of thousands of U.S. combat troops remaining in Iraq for years to come. There is virtually nothing that separates the Democratic Party from the Republican Party when it comes to the issue of Iran, possibly the next "front" in the ongoing "war on terror." None of the "accomplishments" listed by Aumand and Breyman amounted to anything other than what the antiwar movement has been best at doing—orchestrating feel-good events and actions that fail to truly broaden the foundation of the movement, and in the end serve little purpose other than to provide a platform for little more than a continuation of the cycle of self-gratification in the face of defeat. This assessment also applies to the work being done by faith groups and returning servicemen's groups who have taken an antiwar stance. Any movement that operates void of strategic vision, operational direction on how to manifest this strategic vision, and tactical clarity for bringing it all to practical fruition, as well as a unifying organizational structure, is simply wasting time and effort.

If, after all the effort that was put into the multitude of events and activities enumerated by Aumand and Breyman, the momentum toward continuing and expanding war is maintained unchecked, can there be any doubt that the "peace movement" they are involved in is doing anything other than losing? To think or believe otherwise is simply self-delusional. But this seems to be par for the course. After all, Aumand and Breyman noted proudly that "this is one of the—if not *the*—most media-savvy antiwar movements in American history."

Maureen Aumand and Steve Breyman weren't the only ones to take a swing at what I had written. Max Obuszewski, another activist, echoed many similar sentiments when he wrote, "Ritter is a former warrior, and I am a pacifist. I would never tell him how to wage war. And I believe he is out of his element in telling the 'antiwar' movement what it is doing wrong." Another activist, Rachel Treichler, noted that "It sure goes to show that you can take the man out of the army, but you can't take the army out of the man."

But the mother of all responses came from none other than the popular antiwar leader Cindy Sheehan herself. In her article, "The Antiwar Movement," posted on CommonDreams.org on April 7, 2006, Ms. Sheehan lets me have it with both barrels:

> The antiwar movement is not on the "verge of collapse" because we are not organized, or because we don't take a "warrior's" view of attacking the neocons and the war machine using the tactics of Napoleon, or Sun Tzu—but because the two-thirds of Americans who philosophically agree that the war is wrong, BushCo lied, and the troops should come home, will not get off of their collective, complacent, and comfortable behinds to demonstrate their dissent with our government.

"We saw tens of thousands of young people," Sheehan wrote, "take to the streets recently to protests against the proposed election year antics of Congress in their smokescreen of an immigration bill."

> The teens took to the streets because they have something at stake: the very lives of their families. If this bill passes, the families will be split up as their parents are deported back to their countries of origin. The immigrants rightly know that they are being conspired against and that the

only way to stand up for your rights, is to get off of your butt and stand up!

As I reflect on the reality of the U.S. Senate passing the Immigration bill Cindy Sheehan so forcefully condemned, and the fact that this very same bill was signed into law by President Bush in October 2006, I can only wonder if Ms. Sheehan might have had more success had her emotions and deeds been governed less by "get off your butts and stand up!," and more by a systematic approach toward organizing and sustaining a class struggle in the face of genuine ideological warfare.

She certainly did not believe so. "Yes Scott," she wrote, "the antiwar movement is collapsing into a Peace movement. We won't use the tactics of Napoleon, or your hero, Sun Tzu, we will use the tactics of our heroes: Gandhi and Martin Luther King, Jr. Nothing is gained by war, warlike tactics, or warriors, but destruction. Nothing is gained by doing nothing, either. Do something."

Do something. If there ever was a plaintive cry in the dark for help, this is it. Do something. Just don't organize along proven lines for success. Don't think outside of the box that has been constructed by a distinct minority of the public who dominate a movement (whether one calls it "antiwar" or "peace") which should be, and could be, readily embraced by a majority of Americans. In short, don't win. Continue losing. This seems to be what the "antiwar" movement is best at doing. Losing, and rationalizing away their unending string of defeats, and failing to take responsibility for why they are being whipped by their opponents at nearly every turn. Losing has become so prevalent that it seems to have been absorbed into the very essence of the "antiwar" culture.

I admire Gandhi and Martin Luther King. Their passion for peace and justice forever changed the world. But one needs to differentiate between the power of a cult of personality and the power of a systematic approach toward winning. Some may accuse me of being too simplistic. After all, both Martin Luther King and Gandhi possessed formidable leadership and organizational skills. King's efforts propelled American society down the path toward improved civil rights and desegregation and Gandhi was a decisive figure in the movement to evict the British from India. However, I judge people's lasting impact not only on what they did while they were in charge but also on how functional a legacy they left once they disappeared from center stage. A viable organization endures the test of time; the cult of personality collapses when the individual it is built around stumbles or dies. I often wonder how Gandhi would feel about the situation in India today, or what Martin Luther King would say about black political leadership now in America. Neither dream has been well served by its heirs. It is not I who oversimplifies the work of Gandhi or Martin Luther King; it is those in the progressive movement, like Cindy Sheehan, who look to past figures for inspiration void of context.

And thus the danger in waiting for a new messianic figure to emerge and lead the way. Losers wait. Winners do. But "Do Something," without specifying the "what," "why," "when," "who," and "how" is simply a recipe for defeat. While there may be considerable merit in studying the philosophies of Gandhi and Martin Luther King, I would strongly advocate building a framework for lasting operations liberated from the mass appeal of any one individual. Thus, while Sun Tzu and Gandhi may in fact not be mutually exclusive, I will take the Art of War over the teachings of Gandhi any day of the week when looking for a path toward victory. If one wants "inner peace," perhaps Gandhi is your man. In the end, I want to win. That is what warriors do. And who better to teach the art of winning than the warriors themselves?

2

WAGING PEACE

Democracy is an objective. Democratization is a process. Democratization serves the cause of peace because it offers the possibility of justice and of progressive change without force.

—Boutros Boutros-Ghali

* * *

If we accept that life is conflict, and that the objective during conflict is to prevail, then we must speak of waging peace as one would wage war. Peace becomes an objective that must be attained, similar in nature to any military objective sought during war. Do not confuse attaining "inner peace" with achieving a peaceful, nonviolent outcome to a given problem. While I respect pacifists, pacifism in the face of those who oppose you with physical, moral, or ideological violence will only lead to defeat. Our goal and objective is to win, not lose. Only through winning will the antiwar/peace and justice movement see its agenda prevail.

The antiwar movement generally only thrives in a democratic environment, where the rule of law protects those who dissent from official government policy from actual or threatened sanctions, violent or otherwise. It makes little sense talking about growing and sustaining a legitimate antiwar movement, or peace and justice movement, where the rule of law, based upon established principles of democratic governance, does not exist. Therefore, any genuine antiwar/peace and justice movement must first and foremost be a movement that supports democratization as a process, and democracy as an objective.

When waging peace in a democratic environment, it is important to remember that the struggle isn't simply about ideological purity, but more importantly (especially if one is waging peace with an eye on prevailing, and not simply becoming a martyr for a worthwhile, yet futile, cause) that the struggle is a numbers game. Simply put, if the antiwar/peace and justice movement can attract more people to its cause than their opponents can to theirs, then the antiwar/peace and justice movement will emerge victorious. Therefore, a governing principle when waging peace is to create an ideological foundation that is capable of appealing to the broadest possible segment of a given democratic society.

Simplicity is the key. Never forget that the antiwar/peace and justice movement is engaged in a life-or-death struggle with its ideological opponents. Whether these opponents be pro-war, racist, sexist, segregationist, or any other label that one can come up with that signifies an ideology that stands in opposition to the goals and objectives of the antiwar/peace and justice movement, remember this: they have a cause, they have a strategy, and they are fighting to win.

A classic "enemy" in this fight in the name of peace is the so-called religious right. I'm not talking about devout Christians who faithfully practice their religious beliefs, but rather that element which has projected its extremist point of view onto the American scene, injecting God and religion into matters where the United States Constitution says there should be no such role, and professing an intolerance for humanity simply because of creed, race, or other discriminating criteria. The rallying cry of the religious right can be broken down into three words: "Guns, God, and Gays." By promoting such a simplistic agenda, the religious right has been successful in achieving a very broad-spectrum impact on American society, primarily by exploiting the fear that is readily bred through ignorance.

Similar campaigns are run by pro-war/antisocial forces in other democracies around the world. In Australia, Italy, France, Denmark, Sweden, Germany, Austria, Great Britain, and elsewhere, democratic forms of governance serve as vehicles of empowerment for antisocial forces that, like the American religious right, exploit the ignorance of a given population to generate fear, which makes for a more easily manipulated electoral base. At no time will these antisocial forces seek to define their movement and associated activities in a manner that embraces complicated thought or adherence to facts or that otherwise creates the potential to confuse a given audience. Simplicity is the key.

In almost every instance where there is an active antisocial force at play that is prevailing upon the general public, the countervailing antiwar/peace and justice forces have failed to reply with similar simplicity. Instead of three simple words that can be used to capture the imagination (or exploit the ignorance-based fear) of a given audience, the antiwar/peace and justice movements tend to respond with lengthy declarations and statements, which confuse from the outset. An all-too-typical example is one provided by a recent column authored by three visionary California-based "progressive democrats." Published over the internet on December 13, 2006, *Leading "Our" Way: Forward, Together, in the Progressive Movement,* by Wayne Williams, Ahjamu Makalani, and Brad Parker, asks a fundamental question of its audience in its opening paragraph: "Well, here we are Progressive Democrats, sitting on the edge of control, and the responsibility that comes with it. The reins of power that we have fought so long and hard for, power both within the Party and in Washington is near and brings with it a grave responsibility indeed. Will we use it wisely? Will we advance the 'Liberal Ideal'? Will we advance the progressive vision we hold dear in a manner that the American public will not only except, but also embrace?"

Good questions, until the very next passage overwhelms the reader with a plethora of ideas and ideals. "And what is the progressive vision?," the writers ask, before answering with a list that boggles the mind.

- Out of Iraq now and the end to preemptive war.
- Confront Global Warming with the same passion we sustained to go to the moon in the 1960s.
- Establish a sustainable energy future without extractables (oil, coal, uranium and natural gas).
- Investigate & hold accountable those who committed crimes against our nation and humanity—leading to the impeachment of the President and Vice President if necessary.
- Establish Single Payer Universal Health Care.
- Promote Economic Opportunity and Fairness.
- Eliminate the causes of Poverty and alleviate its effects—begin by establishing a living wage for all.
- Bring back fairness to the regressive tax system.
- Rebuild our infrastructure.
- Reestablish our good name in the world by reestablishing dialogue and global cooperation.
- Keep the Internet open and neutral.
- Remove corruption from the political game by moving toward Public Funding of all elections and making sure those elections are transparent, not corporately owned and controlled—have clear auditable paper trails and access to the ballot box for all citizens.

- Promotion of a wider and more diverse news information infrastructure.
- Institute massive structural Prison and Justice Reform in the American Gulag of jails and prisons—immediately abolish the Death Penalty.

"The list goes on and on . . . ," the authors write, which is of course the crux of the problem: Their list goes on and on, and on, and on . . .

"Can we communicate our vision, and conduct our actions in private and in public with the integrity and respect we expected but did not receive from those we have just unseated from power?," they ask. While there is no doubt in my mind that the authors are more than capable of conducting themselves with full honor and integrity, to the first part of their question,—"Can we communicate our vision?"—I can answer straight up: No.

A shopping list of vision will collapse in the face of a simple three-word utterance. "Guns, God, and Gays" will crush the progressive movement's vision every time they come head-to-head in a contest with the religious right for the support of the general public. This vision statement—typical of the progressive movement—is chaotic in its structure, taking the reader across a mind-numbing spectrum of issues, each of which is controversial in its own right. The antisocial forces will have been able to state, and restate, and restate again their fundamental message before the progressives get halfway through their list. And by the time the progressives finish enumerating their vision, the target audience will not have absorbed a single point, making the entire effort moot from the start. Meanwhile, those who were exposed to the antisocial mantra will have no doubt what they have heard. Those who reject such a vision, when offered nothing coherent to counter, will fall into the role of passive or neutral observer and disengage from the process. Those who absorbed the message will become active proponents and defenders, and will be in a better position to explain their vision to an audience than their progressive counterparts.

Vision statements cannot be complicated, especially when trying to expand the base of an organization's membership. Vision statements are not about preaching to the choir. Vision statements must be concise and to the point, in addition to remaining true to the ideals and values of a given organization. The religious right in America has a very complex social agenda that goes well beyond the bounds set by the simple "Guns, God, and Gays" rallying cry. But in order to win over a majority of the electoral support in a democratic form of governance, they have parsed their public vision into the right to bear arms, the moral ascendancy of God (and in particular, a Christian God) in the daily lives of all Americans, and the definition of marriage as a union between a man and a woman. From these three core principles can be extracted numerous other vision statements, but these will be put on hold until the religious right achieves its electoral victory. At that time the ghosts of their overall agenda will emerge from the shadows, to be pursued aggressively without the immediate recourse to a general vote.

The antiwar/peace and justice movement needs to simplify its message in a similar fashion. This must be done in a way that isn't only for the edification of the antiwar/peace and justice community, but with an eye toward achieving majority support among the general public. Waging peace means waging an all-out fight for public opinion. This is best achieved through the sage marketing of one's own ideas and values, and not simply by attacking the deficiencies in those of the opposition.

Streamlining the message also means streamlining the messenger. A couple of facts need to be examined. The antiwar/peace and justice movement, and the entire progressive movement in America for that matter, represents a distinct minority in the United States today. It would be a mistake to assess the November 2006 mid-term elections as representing a victory for progressive policies. Nothing could be further from the truth. The Democrats won because more Americans were against the policies of the Bush administration, not because these same voters were for the "vision" expressed by the progressives.

In order for the antiwar/peace and justice movement to succeed, those who seek to wage peace need to understand that in the end victory will come only if they successfully craft a message, combined with a messenger vehicle, that is attractive to the majority of Americans. The current face of the antiwar/peace and justice movement is not the face of mainstream America. This is not a bad thing, just a reality check. If mainstream America examines the antiwar/peace and justice movement, and cannot identify with it in terms of message and membership, then there is no chance of success. "Mainstream" will not convert into "Progressive." In order to win, "Progressive" must morph itself into "Mainstream," or a close facsimile thereof.

This is a difficult task for a movement that prides itself on being inclusive and "democratic" in nature. But the fact is that there are elements against the progressive movement that serve to create friction within mainstream America when it comes to the antiwar/peace and justice message. In order to succeed in waging a battle of ideas and ideals among the larger American public, those who battle under the banner of the progressive movement need to establish a core value that is not only marketable to the majority of Americans but also unquestionably accepted by those who wage peace in its cause.

When I was a chief inspector with the United Nations, I had the task of assembling weapons inspectors from around the world, representing a multitude of ethnicities, professional experiences, personalities, and political beliefs. There was neither time nor inclination to build a team that was all-inclusive of each individual's personal desire. I had to identify a center of gravity around which to build the team, and give it well-defined core values. I did this by making the implementation of Security Council resolutions regarding Iraq's disarmament of weapons of mass destruction the only priority for the team.

I did not care what the positions of the French, British, Russian, or American governments were at the time, or what the personal beliefs of the individual inspectors might be. They needed to sign on to my declared set of values, and pursue the implementation of these values with a single-minded purpose during the course of the inspection. Any inspector who deviated from this core value system was free to go home. As a result of this process, I was able to build inspection teams with an unmatched record of performance and dependability under pressure. The loyalty and integrity of these inspection teams set a standard that often dictated the nature of international action with respect to Iraq. We inspectors were not waging war, nor were we waging peace. We were waging inspections, and we played the game to win.

The antiwar/peace and justice movement needs to play to win as well, and as such needs to build a team capable of winning. The first step is to define a center of gravity, a core value or belief that is easily and simply expressed by those marketing it, and understood by those receiving it. A good benchmark to use in doing this is what I call the "firefighter standard." I choose firefighters not only because I have a soft spot for them in my heart (and, in the spirit of full disclosure, serve as a volunteer firefighter in my home town of Delmar, New York), but also because if you are trying to market something to mainstream America, if you can sell it to firefighters, whose profession is ranked number one in terms of jobs that garner the respect of the general public, then you can sell it to the majority of Americans as well.

Firefighters are, believe it or not, the natural allies of the peace and justice movement, and by extension, the antiwar movement. Firefighters represent the first line of defense for a community when things go really bad. In responding to fires, accidents, hazardous conditions, and medical emergencies, firefighters know more about the reality of their community than just about anyone. They know where the slumlords reign, because they've had to tackle the problems created with overcrowding and poverty. Firefighters know where the dregs of society accumulate; whether it be the drunks, drug dealers, prostitutes, or runaways, the firefighters know because they are the ones who give these people care when they need it most. Need to organize around immigration issues in your community? The firefighter will be able to tell you where the Somalis are, the Mexicans, the Albanians, the Greeks, the Russians, and any other ethnic group you may have in mind.

More so than even the police, the firefighters understand the dark underside of society because they don't simply confront it, they try to help it. You don't have to work hard to convince a firefighter that there is a problem in his or her respective community. They know this all too well. However, one needs to tread softly when discussing these matters. While never shy when it comes to criticizing politicians who fail to do their jobs, firefighters bristle when the criticism crosses the line into what they feel to be an attack on their own core values, which tend to revolve around love of country and community. As members of a service institution, firefighters are very close to the armed forces. They don't brook those who criticize the men and women who serve our nation in the military. They are respectful of the rule of law, and have little tolerance for those who seek to break it. They tend to be type A personalities who seek to solve problems through action and not words. Endless meetings for meetings' sake, or holding vigils, or participating in demonstrations would not necessarily be the activities one associates with the fire service and those who work within it.

One would not necessarily think of a firefighter when examining the makeup of your average progressive/antiwar/peace and justice gathering, despite the fact that they share a similar concern for the welfare of the community. Nothing highlighted this reality more than the World Trade Organization demonstrations that hit Seattle, Washington, in 1999. While the Seattle police department responded to a mostly peaceful demonstration with alarming brutality and excessive force, the Seattle fire department showed why firefighters remain among society's most respected servants. When ordered by the mayor of Seattle to turn their fire hoses against the crowds of demonstrators in order to disperse them, the firefighters refused, and in some cases stood side by side with the demonstrators, arms folded in defiance.

Win over the firefighters, and you win over society. The firefighters in Seattle responded the way they did not because they shared the anti–World Trade Organization agenda of the demonstrators, but because they are "rule of law" Americans who refuse to trample on the basic rights of the demonstrators in the exercise of their freedom of speech. This basic right is derived from a single document, the Constitution of the United States of America. I couldn't think of a better core value for the progressive movement to declare as their own than the ideals and values that are set forth in the Constitution. From the standpoint of the United States, this document defines who we are and what we are as a people. Its preamble, beginning as it does with the words, "We the People," provides both the certificate of ownership of the ideals and values for all Americans and the call for each American citizen to live up to the challenge of government "of the people, by the people, and for the people," as so eloquently stated by President Abraham Lincoln in his Gettysburg Address.

If the progressive/antiwar/peace and justice movement wants to successfully confront the "Guns, God, and Gays" message of the religious right, or the equally vile rhetorical messages of any other antisocial movement in America or around the world, then there is no better rallying point than around the Constitution of the United States, with its message of "Freedom and Justice for All." There is nothing more American than to embrace the Constitution of the United States and what it stands for. From within this document comes all that progressives could ever hope to stand for. Every single "vision" point embraced by progressives can be traced back to the Constitution and what it stands for. Imagine sitting down across a "Guns, God, and Gays" religious-rights advocate, tossing down a copy of the Constitution, and challenging him or her to find any mention of God.

The Constitution, as Chief Justice John Marshall affirmed in writing his many landmark opinions, emanated not from a state or states, but rather from a free and sovereign people. "We the People" are the sovereign protectors of the Constitution's authority and viability. If one were to reflect on the level of knowledge that exists in America today about the Constitution, the results would be shocking. I am often asked to speak before high school and college audiences. Each time I ask for a show of hands of those who have read the Constitution. The number of respondents is always depressingly low, generally no more than 10 percent of the audience. The results are no better (and indeed, often worse) when this same question is posed to middle-aged and elderly audiences.

Patriotism may be in vogue, but patriotism void of a sound ideological foundation is nothing more than empty bluster. One cannot genuinely act as a functioning citizen of the United States if one hasn't read, comprehended, and absorbed into one's daily life the ideals and values set forth in the Constitution of the United States. There simply is no other measurement of what it means to be an

American. If you haven't read the Constitution (and it appears that most Americans have not), then you're not a functioning American. How can "We the People" possibly serve as the sovereign protectors of the Constitution if we don't even know anything about the document and the ideals and values contained within that serve to define who we are and what we are as a people?

The Constitution, like the soul of America, lies discarded and trampled by those who would seek to hijack the promise of America for their own self-serving purposes. It is because of this that the religious right and their ilk can get away with their patently un-American "Guns, Gods, and Gays" rallying theme. If progressives are truly interested in waging peace, and fighting to win, then they will pick up the banner of the Constitution and claim it as their own, and make their rallying cry, one that is derived from the very essence of that which defines this great nation. A pro-Constitution movement would do more to further the cause of the progressive/antiwar/peace and justice movement than anything else, and would be extremely attractive to mainstream America, the battle for whose support the ideological struggle for the future of America hinges on. If the progressive/antiwar/peace and justice movement would take up this task, it would stand a good chance at success. Just ask a firefighter.

* * *

*See **Appendix A** for a copy of the Constitution of the United States. Read it. Understand it. Live it. And above all else, defend it.*

3

THE ART OF WAR

The quickest way of ending a war is to lose it.

—George Orwell

* * *

Many people, including a number of my critics in the progressive movement, have indicated that my ready embrace of the so-called Art of War is an automatic by-product of my being an officer of Marines, as if a certificate for this subject was handed out along with my lieutenant's bars. Nothing could be further from the truth. My embrace of the Art of War came as a result of a personal journey facilitated by, but not necessarily fully endorsed by, my service in the Marines. This journey represented an awakening of consciousness about conflict and how it should be waged when one is called upon to do so. It is my hope that each reader of this book will undertake a similar journey (recognizing that each individual circumstance will differ) in which the Art of War is discovered and brought into relevance. For the purpose of illustrating how such a journey might unfold, I will share with the reader my own story.

I was commissioned as a second lieutenant in the United States Marine Corps upon graduation from Franklin and Marshall College, on a sunny day in late May 1984. I had been preparing for this moment for many years, first (and perhaps unconsciously) as a career air force officer's son who grew up on military bases across the United States and around the world. I have memories of my father deploying to Vietnam early in my childhood, and my high school years were spent moving from the warm tropics of Hickam Air Force Base in Hawaii to Balgat Air Base in Ankara, Turkey (where my father served as an advisor to the Turkish Air Force), and then to Sembach Air Force Base in the Rhein-Pfalz region of what was then West Germany.

I had known nothing other than the life of a military family, so it was no great surprise that my goals and ambitions in life were defined by the military. I wrestled with exactly which branch I wanted to serve in, gravitating from the Coast Guard (they did their real jobs even in times of peace) to the air force, then the army (I actually enlisted in the army after high school, spending a year at the West Point Preparatory School in Fort Monmouth, New Jersey before deciding the army wasn't for me after all) before finally deciding on the Marine Corps.

The Marine Corps had everything I was looking for in the military—esprit de corps, tradition, and a reputation of being the very best. The motto popular in Marine Corps recruiting circles at the time was "We Never Promised You a Rose Garden," complemented by "If Everyone Could Be a Marine, There Wouldn't Be a Marine Corps." The working assumption was that the Marine Corps, unlike the other branches of the armed forces at the time, set its own standards, which were uncompromising and unsympathetic to those who couldn't measure up. I was attracted by the notion of belonging to a very select group that was confident in the fact that it could kick the hell out of anyone who dared get in its way.

I arrived in Quantico, Virginia, in November 1984 with all of the confidence that spending two summers in that corner of

Northern Virginia, six weeks at a time, in platoon leader's course (PLC) could engender. I had experienced the hell of Camp Upshur, where marine sergeants and corporals took perverse thrill in breaking the bodies and spirit of the soft, elitist college boys who kept showing up every summer thinking they had what it took to be an officer of Marines. Camp Brown was only marginally better, if only because by then the college boys had become college men, and were slightly more prepared for the even more grueling physical and mental challenges being placed before them.

At PLC we had been lowly officer candidates. When I arrived in Quantico, Virginia, in the fall of 1984, I was a bona fide officer of Marines, with nice shiny golden bars on my shoulders to prove it. The Marine Corps spent the next six months putting me through the paces of the basic school, where all marine lieutenants, regardless of their military occupation specialty (pilot, infantry, artillery, intelligence, administration, and so on) learned first and foremost to be rifle platoon commanders. In addition to honing my skills as a novice warrior, TBS proved to me that I had much left to learn about being an officer in this institution known as the United States Marine Corps.

I graduated from TBS in May 1985, and was assigned to the Marine Corps Air Ground Combat Center in Twenty-nine Palms, California, as a intelligence officer to the 7th Marine Amphibious Brigade (MAB), the primary combat element of the Marine Corps' force allocation for what was known as the "Rapid Deployment Force," or RDF, an outgrowth of the so-called Carter Doctrine, which came into being following the Soviet invasion of Afghanistan in 1979. The RDF was designed to project U.S. military power into Southwest Asia, including the oil-rich environs of the Middle East.

* * *

At the time of my assignment to the 7th MAB, the RDF had its hands full, preparing to deal with Soviet incursions into Iran from its forward bases in Afghanistan, and dealing in turn with the possible threat of an Iranian breakthrough on the southern front around the Iraqi city of Basra, where major battles in the nearly seven-year war between Iran and Iraq threatened not only the rich oil fields of southern Iraq but also those of neighboring Kuwait and Saudi Arabia. In addition, the 7th MAB had responsibility for reinforcing NATO's northern flank, around Denmark and northern Germany, in case of conflict with the Soviet Union.

Whether as a MAB, or as part of a larger Marine Amphibious Force (MAF, built around a Marine Division–Air Wing combat team), the forces available to the marine component of the Rapid Deployment Force numbered between 10,000 and 30,000 marines. From my perspective an intelligence officer assigned to reviewing and updating contingency plans for war, it became clear that the marines would be fighting an enemy that outnumbered them on a scale of 5:1 to more than 10:1. The days of storming the beach Iwo Jima–style were long gone. Heroics of that sort would only guarantee that the Marine Corps would be defeated on the field of battle. In order to face this new military reality, the Marine Corps needed a new approach to fighting war.

While I was sweating it out in the woods around northern Virginia between November 1984 and May 1985, the Marine Corps was undergoing a revolution in military thought. Under the leadership of an innovative marine general, Al Gray, the Marine Corps Combat Development Command in Quantico sought to redefine how marines would wage war in the coming years. As new lieutenants, my peers and I were voracious readers of the *Marine Corps Gazette,* the professional journal of the Marine Corps Association. There, in the pages of this magazine, we were exposed to a whole new way of thinking, so-called maneuver warfare, which based its theory and underlying philosophy on the German "Storm Trooper" tactics of World War One and the Blitzkrieg operations of World War Two.

The theorists who wrote about maneuver warfare sprinkled their articles liberally with German words and phrases, leading to much derisive mocking on the part of the all-wise lieutenants. In our arrogance, we believed we knew what maneuver warfare was. After all, we were an amphibious force, training to fight "from the sea," as it were. The history of the Marine Corps was replete with examples of how those who had gone before us had successfully plied our trade: the island-hopping campaign in the Pacific during World War Two, in which we bypassed the major Japanese defenses by hitting less-well-defended islands. And every marine knows the story of the Inchon landings, during the Korean War, where the 1st Marine Division thrust into the rear area of the North Koreans, prompting the collapse of the North Korean military and their retreat from South Korean soil.

We lieutenants did not need to hear about German fighting methods (after all, we had defeated the Germans in both wars, had we not?). We were the proud heirs of a military tradition that had prevailed in every battle it had fought in. Our only "defeat" came at the hands of army and navy superiors who ordered marines to lay down their arms in Corregidor and Wake Island at a time when marines were more than holding their own against the enemy.

Like other lieutenants, I was a big fan of aggressive tactics. Find the enemy, fix the enemy, and destroy the enemy through firepower and maneuver. But not the high-minded maneuver of William Lind and Colonel Michael Wyly, who were expounding their theories in the *Marine Corps Gazette,* but rather the time-tested Marine Corps maneuver of a right or left envelopment (maneuvering around the flanks of an enemy position), or failing that, my all-time favorite, the frontal assault. There wasn't a tactical problem that could not be overcome simply by laying down a heavy base of fire and charging through the enemy position.

Fortunately for us lieutenants, we were placed under the guidance of captains who had cut their tactical teeth under the leadership of General Al Gray. These captains watched our "heroics" in the bloodless woods of Quantico, and then quietly yet firmly helped show us the errors of our ways. We soon learned that we were stuck in the past, in effect refighting the last American war in Vietnam, and not preparing for the realities of the new modern battlefield. Our passion for assaulting the enemy belied the reality that we were trapped in rigid thinking. We didn't move until told to move. We didn't deviate from the mission orders, regardless of what was happening. Told to take the hill, we took the hill, at all costs. And sometimes those costs were exorbitant.

Slowly yet effectively, our captains won us over to a new way of thinking. We learned about understanding the commander's "intent," so that we knew the reason behind taking the hill, and allowed the mission objective (for instance, "interdict enemy supply lines") to influence us, as opposed to a piece of terrain ("take the hill"). We learned that the reason for taking the hill was that it provided dominating terrain from which a given trail or road could be interdicted. However, if when taking the hill we were faced with overwhelming enemy resistance, or if the enemy shifted its supply routes from one road to another, we had the flexibility to modify our actions accordingly, so that we accomplished the commander's intent of interdicting enemy supply lines without taking the hill.

* * *

Sometimes we had to be reined in by the captains, because in our exuberant embrace of "commander's intent" we found ourselves being transformed from a structured, disciplined force of marines into a mob of enthusiastic individualists, each of us running around the woods looking more like Rambo than a U.S. marine. The captains allowed us to move from one extreme to another, until by the time we graduated from TBS we had become not only the hardened, disciplined leaders of men that any former marine would have readily recognized but also intellectually awakened military theorists who devoured everything we could get our hands on regarding the Art of War.

Two books in particular were made mandatory reading by the Marine Corps leadership: the Chinese military philosopher Sun Tzu's *The Art of War,* and the Prussian General Carl von Clausewitz's *On War.* It was not uncommon to see marine lieutenants nursing their beers around the bar at an Officer's Club on a Friday night debating the relative merits of the mystical subtleties of a sixth-century Chinese warlord and the brute-force approach of an early nineteenth-century contemporary of Napoleon Bonaparte.

We discussed the maddening, yet sage, "yin and yang" philosophical statements of Sun Tzu. My personal favorite, as an intelligence officer, was "All warfare is based on deception. Hence, when able to attack, we must seem unable; when using our forces, we must seem inactive; when we are near, we must make the enemy believe we are far away; when far away, we must make him believe we are near. Hold out baits to entice the enemy. Feign disorder, and crush him." Others chose the more brutally straightforward pronouncements of Clausewitz, such as this gem: "If the enemy is to be coerced, you must put him in a situation that is even more unpleasant than the sacrifice you call on him to make. The hardships of the situation must not be merely transient—at least not in appearance. Otherwise, the enemy would not give in, but would wait for things to improve."

We were no longer simply satisfied with perfecting a given

war-fighting skill, such as the tactical employment of a rifle platoon in an urban assault, or positioning an artillery battery to most effectively provide fire support to a designated unit. We sought perspective, and, along with that, vision. We moved beyond being mere pawns on the field of battle, instead seeking to understand a potential conflict in its entirety, so that we might more effectively render our responsibilities as a part of that whole. Recognizing our limitations as mere lieutenants, we never sought to usurp authority, but rather complement it by being better prepared to execute, in context, that which we were charged with implementing.

In 1987 General Al Gray became the commandant of the Marine Corps, and with that promotion maneuver warfare went from being some dark art taught to young lieutenants by maverick captains to becoming the warrior philosophy of the United States Marine Corps. General Gray visited 29 Palms and summoned the lieutenants to an auditorium, where he put us on notice as to what he expected from us. "You are the future of the Marine Corps," he said. "Act like it matters to you." He challenged us professionally, and being the professionals we were, we took it personally.

As an intelligence officer recently assigned to an artillery battalion, I was immediately put to the test. Most marine officers in the combat arms (infantry, artillery, armor) embraced a variant of maneuver warfare, focusing on those aspects that highlighted their particular specialty. Unfortunately, many of these became overly focused on simply the "maneuver" facet, failing to integrate into their mode of operations the full spectrum of the various factors influencing the overall battlefield. I watched as senior operations officers became married to a given plan, whether or not the terrain on which it was being executed was conducive to that course of action.

And when it came to intelligence on the enemy, these combat arms officers were almost derisive in their rejection of "analysis" having any role on the front lines of combat. "The best intelligence

I gather is from the tip of my bayonet," one lieutenant colonel told me once as I tried to explain the need to find out more about what the opponent was up to before we began executing our plan.

If I invoked the Art of War in theory, they loved coming back at me with a quote from Clausewitz: "Many intelligence reports in war are contradictory; even more are false, and most are uncertain." Of course, I had a Sun Tzu quote ready in response: "Intelligence is the most important work, because the entire force relies on it for every move." While my Sun Tzu may have trumped their Clausewitz, their major oak leaves trumped my lieutenant bars every single time, with one exception: according to the Marine Corps Command and Staff Manual, I was a staff officer with equal access and standing before the battalion commander.

Emboldened by General Gray's challenge, I elevated the matter directly to my battalion commander, an innovative thinker named Nick Carlucci. "And what should your role be, Lieutenant?," he asked me. "Intelligence drives operations, sir," was my response. "I need to be fully integrated into what we do as a battalion." Colonel Carlucci agreed, as did his successor, Colonel Chase. I was tasked with developing a strategic training plan that would help focus our battalion's operations on fighting a Soviet-style enemy who outnumbered us significantly. Exercises were conducted that focused on combining speed and maneuverability with an improved ability to collect information on the enemy's disposition and intent, and to interdict such with the timely application of firepower. We worked hand in hand with infantry, armor, and air power to maximize the synergy created when utilizing combined arms. In short, we became the best field artillery unit in the entire Marine Corps, and if given the chance to prove it, I would bet the entire western world.

In 1988 I was transferred from my assignment as a battalion intelligence officer to a new job as an inspector charged with the implementation of the Intermediate Nuclear Forces Treaty, the

1987 agreement between the United States and the Soviet Union to eliminate their entire inventories of intermediate- and short-range ballistic missiles. I continued my aggressive pursuit of having intelligence fully integrated into every aspect of an operation, and as a result had a profound impact on how the United States conducted itself in arms control and disarmament activities with the Soviet Union. While my work in the Soviet Union had little to do with the wartime mission of the Marine Corps, it did increase my confidence as an intelligence officer, and in the important role intelligence played in the overall concept of operations, and indeed, strategy.

My tour in the Soviet Union ended in July 1990. In August 1990 Saddam Hussein invaded Kuwait, and America found itself preparing for war with Iraq. As someone who had written a paper on Iraqi defensive combat back when I covered the Iran-Iraq War for the 7th Marine Amphibious Brigade, my services in support of helping prepare for war with Iraq were suddenly in demand. I was pulled from my seat at the Amphibious Warfare School in Quantico, Virginia (the professional-level school for captains) and assigned to an entity known as the "Ad Hoc Study Group," formed under the direct orders of General Al Gray as a means of devising innovative force employment options for Marine Corps units in support of any war with Iraq.

General Gray had taken his vision of maneuver warfare and turned it into official Marine Corps doctrine. He assisted in the preparation of a new Fleet Marine Force Manual, FMFM-1, *Warfighting,* which was published in 1989. This document became required reading for all marines, and I for one devoured it with all the enthusiasm a true believer could muster. Having been an active participant both in the development of the philosophical underpinnings of maneuver warfare in the classrooms and forests of Quantico, Virginia, and its operational application in the deserts of

29 Palms, California, I immediately grasped the significance of this new doctrine. "Maneuver warfare," General Gray wrote, "is a warfighting philosophy that seeks to shatter the enemy's cohesion through a variety of rapid, focused, and unexpected actions which create a turbulent and rapidly deteriorating situation with which the enemy cannot cope." This was my kind of thinking, and I felt history had delivered me to the exact position I needed to be in through my assignment with the Ad Hoc Study Group.

However, as the junior officer on this team, I feared my voice would be suppressed by the sheer presence of senior rank. Fortunately, the man overseeing the Ad Hoc Study Group, Colonel Michael Steele, and his boss, Major General Matthew Caulfield, were innovative thinkers in their own right, and anyone who had something to contribute to the mission was given equal opportunity to express it. A number of options were developed, including my own concept of inserting marine forces into the rear areas of the Iraqi Army at a critical juncture in the ground attack phase of the operation. The Iraqis had built considerable defenses along the Kuwaiti–Saudi Arabian border. Behind these defenses they had arrayed their strategic reserve, the Republican Guard armored and mechanized divisions. General Norman Schwarzkopf, the commander of U.S. forces in the region, had already identified the Iraqi Republican Guard as representing the "center of gravity" of Saddam Hussein's regime. As such, in order to defeat Saddam, the Republican Guard must be defeated.

The plan of action as devised by General Schwarzkopf and his army planners was to have the Marine Corps engage the Iraqi Army along the length of its defensive positions, freezing them in place while the army forces swung around to the west, outflanking the Iraqi defenses and moving in to engage and destroy the Republican Guard. There were numerous problems with this plan. First of all, it had the Marine Corps forgoing an attempt at exploiting its penchant for maneuver warfare, and simply conducting a frontal assault in the teeth of the Iraqi defenses. Second, the army would simply be maneuvering to engage the Republican Guard in a classic battle of attrition, with no effort made to divert Iraqi attention away from the main effort or to place the Iraqi forces in a quandary, by presenting them with two simultaneous threats—to react to one exposes them to defeat by the other, and vice versa. In short, everything we as marines had been training to do when it came to warfare was being thrown out the window.

General Gray did his best to rectify this situation. In a dramatic briefing in his office at Headquarters Marine Corps, the Ad Hoc Study Team presented the commandant with our plan to launch marine amphibious forces into the rear of the Republican Guard at the same time the army was maneuvering in from the west to engage them. If the Republican Guard reacted to our assault from the sea by turning about and engaging us, then the army would close in on them from behind and annihilate them. If the Iraqis failed to respond to the marine attack, focusing instead on taking on the army, then we marines would cut off the Iraqi lines of communication, close in behind them, and annihilate them. In any event, the Republican Guard would be destroyed, the Iraqi center of gravity eliminated, and Saddam Hussein's regime finished.

Although I was the author of the plan, as a junior my role in presenting the concept was limited to flipping the slides I had painstakingly designed. With the briefing over, and the floor opened to discussion, the Marine Corps commandant turned to me and asked if I had any comments. "You look like a smart young man," he said, "and I don't think they brought you here just to flip slides." I told General Gray that I believed if we executed this plan, then the Marine Corps would spend more time processing prisoners than fighting the Republican Guard. "The Iraqis do not operate effectively when their command and control is degraded, and with this operation, we will eviscerate their command and control. I think the battle will be over even before it truly begins. This plan represents the epitome of maneuver warfare."

General Gray agreed, and approved the plan as briefed, but efforts to get General Schwarzkopf to adopt it were unsuccessful. The army plan went forward, with the Marine Corps fighting through the Iraqi defenses to take Kuwait City, and the army sweeping around the west flank to engage the Republican Guard. While bloodied, the Iraqi Republican Guard was never decisively engaged, and managed to survive the war intact, ensuring Saddam Hussein's continued survival for more than a decade to come. In the years that passed, I had numerous opportunities to discuss the war with Iraqi Republican Guard officers. They were convinced that they had won, because the United States, not they, had initiated the ceasefire that brought hostilities to an end. The ceasefire kept the Republican Guard intact, and these units went on to violently suppress the uprising of the Kurds in northern Iraq and the Shia revolt in southern Iraq. We had failed to accomplish our mission of destroying Saddam's center of gravity. In retrospect, I would have to say that the Iraqi point of view about the war's victor had some merit.

I have been frustrated ever since the unsatisfactory end of the first Gulf War in 1991 by the inability, and seeming unwillingness, of my fellow military professionals in the army, air force, and navy to embrace maneuver warfare as a war-winning doctrine. My military career ended shortly after the fighting stopped, and I went on to join the United Nations as a weapons inspector. One could imagine my journey of discovery of the Art of War to have reached its natural conclusion, however frustrating it was personally. But my curiosity as to why the Marine Corps way of waging war was not being readily adopted by our fellow services prompted me to dig deeper into the philosophical roots of General Al Gray's *Warfighting* vision.

What I found astounded me: the father of modern maneuver warfare wasn't a marine after all. It wasn't a Chinese warlord, or a Prussian general. He was an air force colonel named John Boyd, and his notions of conflict would revolutionize my attitudes toward not only warfare but also any clash of competing forces, whether they be martial or ideological.

4

Decision Making

In a moment of decision, the best thing you can do is the right thing to do. The worst thing you can do is nothing.

—Theodore Roosevelt

* * *

John Boyd was a fighter pilot during the Korean War. He studied aerial warfare like no other had done before him, examining the tactics and machinery of air-to-air combat over the course of history. His intimate knowledge and insight gained through this examination of how aircraft behave led him to the conclusion that in aerial combat, there are but a finite number of maneuvers, and responses to maneuvers, that are capable of being performed. Furthermore, his investigations into what is known as "energy-maneuverability" demonstrated that a given aircraft's performance could be quantitatively measured in terms of kinetic and potential energy throughout its flight envelope. These measurements in turn could be used to compare the relative performance of one aircraft against any other type of aircraft.

In short, aerial combat was all about the "knowns"—how an aircraft performs, and how a pilot can maneuver. By knowing and understanding the competing performance characteristics of his own and an opponent's aircraft, a good pilot would be able to force a situation to his advantage by executing a quick series of maneuvers that were designed to exploit the performance characteristics of his own plane, while compelling his opponent to respond in a predictable manner that would then be exploited so that the well-trained pilot would always end up in an advantageous position—meaning he would shoot down his opponent.

In his seminal work, *Patterns of Conflict* (taken from a 1986 slide presentation he put together), Boyd stated that in aerial combat the ideal would be "a fighter that can both lose energy and gain energy more quickly while out-turning an adversary. In other words, suggest a fighter that can pick and choose engagement opportunities, and yet has fast transients ('buttonhook') characteristics that can be used to either force an overshoot by an attacker or stay inside a hard turning defender."

The idea of "fast transients," according to Boyd, centered on the notion that "in order to win, we should operate at a faster tempo or rhythm than our adversaries—or, better yet, get inside the adversary's Observation-Orientation-Decision-Action time cycle or loop."This was the initial presentation of what has famously become known as the OODA-Loop. "Such activity," Boyd writes, "will make us appear ambiguous (unpredictable) thereby generating confusion and disorder among our adversaries—since our adversaries will be unable to generate mental images or pictures that agree with the menace as well as faster transient rhythm or patterns they are competing against."

The goal of the OODA-Loop, according to Boyd, is to "simultaneously compress our own time and stretch out adversary time to generate a favorable mismatch in time/ability to shape and adapt to change." "One's time" is in effect dependent upon one's ability to formulate and execute decisions. As such, the key to victory, according to Boyd, is to shorten one's own decision-making cycle while increasing that of one's opponent, to "get inside the decision-making cycle of the enemy."

Boyd didn't simply derive the OODA-Loop for utilization in air-to-air combat. He viewed the decision-making cycle as possessing discernable characteristics drawn from his study of the essence of human nature. Boyd believed that life was, in essence, conflict, and that there were general characteristics common to those who, over the course of time and history, prevailed in conflict. These included the need to possess "a variety of responses that can be applied rapidly to gain sustenance, avoid danger, and diminish adversary's capacity for independent action," the need for organizations or groups to "cooperate or, better yet, harmonize their activities in their endeavors to survive as an organic synthesis," and that in order "to shape and adapt to change one cannot be passive; instead one must take the initiative." These four qualities—variety, rapidity, harmony, and initiative—are what Boyd terms "key qualities that permit one to shape and adapt to an ever-changing environment." In short, those who possess the qualities of variety/rapidity/harmony/initiative will function on a much tighter decision-making cycle, or OODA-Loop, than their opponent.

What Boyd called "transients" from an energy-maneuverability standpoint, Sun Tzu in *The Art of War* called the *Chen* and *Chi* of combat—in short, a situation in which *Chen* maneuvers exposed an adversary's weaknesses, which were then exploited by a decisive stroke, or *Chi*. Boyd spent a great deal of time in *Patterns of Conflict* discussing the *Chen* and *Chi* of Sun Tzu, in a historical context, citing examples of decisive maneuvering in battle over the years. Much of Boyd's thesis concerning the qualities of the variety/rapidity/harmony/initiative collective is derived from the philosophies of conflict set forth by Sun Tzu.

Boyd studied many military theoreticians, including Napoleon and his Prussian adversarial contemporary, Carl von Clausewitz. Boyd was impressed with some of Clausewitz's points, especially those that reinforced his notion of the so-called organic synthesis collective (variety/rapidity/harmony/initiative). Important among these were the concept of "will," and the definition of war as a continuation of politics and policy that sought to use violence to impose one's will upon another. The oft-quoted "War is nothing more than the continuation of politics by other means" has been misrepresented by many critics of Clausewitz who feel the Prussian general was imposing linear rationality (given the tendency of most to willingly substitute "politics," a process that combines the rational with the irrational, with "policy," which is in effect rational action taken by a group possessing power in order to maintain or expand that power) on a distinctly nonlinear concept called "war." Few who quote Clausewitz have read Clausewitz. If they did, they would see the Prussian expands further on this matter in a way that brings more clarity to his description of the nonlinear, emotional aspects of war as politics. "If war is part of politics, politics will determine its character. As politics becomes more ambitious and vigorous, so will war, and this may reach the point where war attains its absolute form. . . . Politics is the guiding intelligence and war only the instrument, not vice versa." Now substitute, as many have, "policy" for "politics," and see what happens to the meaning of the passage. Thus, when Clausewitz states, "War is an act of force to compel our enemy to do our will," he isn't simply speaking of the violent act of physical combat, but the more emotional and moral amalgamation of conflict that defines "politics," a complicated process, versus "policy," a rational expression of politics.

Clausewitz discussed the existence of "friction," noting that the interaction of many factors serves as an impediment to activity. Uncertainty was such a factor, as were the effects of psychological and moral forces. Some refer to this as the "fog of war." Clausewitz was more descriptive: "We have identified danger, physical exertion, intelligence, *and friction* as the elements that coalesce to form *the atmosphere* of war, and turn it into a medium that impedes activity." Sun Tzu covered the spiritual aspects of war; Clausewitz focused on the emotional. Clausewitz held that the harmonious balance of mind and temperament enabled one to overcome the friction generated from the complex actions of conflict. "War is the realm of uncertainty," Clausewitz wrote. "Two qualities are indispensable: first, an intellect that, even in the darkest hour, retains some glimmerings of the inner light which leads to truth; and second, the courage to follow this faint light wherever it may lead." These "qualities" were something Boyd adopted in his "organic synthesis" collective.

Boyd was critical of Clausewitz, however, when it came to the military application of his theory of war in actual combat, noting that in the end the Clausewitzian model of war was little more than glorified conflict through attrition, a reworking of Napoleonic warfare in its latter stages. Eventually, Boyd returned to the principles of Sun Tzu, worked through a modern German medium in which *Chen* became *Nebenpunkt* and *Chi* transformed into *Schwerpunkt*. The language changed, but the principles remained the same: maneuver your opponent into a position where his weaknesses are exposed, and then exploit these weaknesses with a well-timed decisive blow. But we now see, through an understanding of Clausewitz, that this maneuver can be political as well as physical, invoking the moral and intellectual as well as brute force.

To Boyd, success in conflict—military, business, or other—could be boiled down into this simple statement: "He who is willing and able to take the initiative to exploit variety, rapidity, and harmony—as the basis to create as well as adapt to the more indistinct—more irregular—quicker changes of rhythm and pattern, yet shape the focus and direction of effort—survives and dominates." Likewise, the opposite held true: "He who is unwilling or unable to take the initiative to exploit variety, rapidity, and harmony . . . goes under or survives to be dominated."

The key to all of this is to understand the concept of friction and its role in the decision-making cycle. By employing *variety* and *rapidity* in one's operations, an adversary's own friction is increased, thereby delaying his ability to respond to a given situation. The use of *harmony* and *initiative* enables one to reduce one's own friction, thereby increasing one's own ability to make decisions that exploit inherent strengths exhibited through *variety* and *rapidity* in operations.

The "organic synthesis" collective of *variety/rapidity* and *harmony/initiative* concepts combine to enable one to conduct decision making in a much more dynamic, efficient manner than one's opponent. Once you operate inside (i.e., quicker than) an opponent's decision-making cycle (i.e., the OODA-Loop), the resulting friction creates uncertainty, confusion, doubt, disorder, fear, panic, and, ultimately, chaos, which will paralyze an opponent into indecision and defeat.

This is the essence of Boyd.

The key is in the execution of the OODA-Loop (see page 103). The first element of this "loop" is *Observation,* which involves seeing, sensing, and comprehending one's environment. From a human perspective, this is a difficult element to quantify, simply because of the need to repeat consistent and objective observations, which are virtually impossible to accomplish when involving humans. It is essential, therefore, when conducting the *Observation* element of the OODA-Loop, to be intimately aware of any factors that might have a bearing on your ability to rationally assess a situation, and ideally to possess similar insight into limitations (or lack thereof) on the part of your opponent.

Next is *Orientation,* which is perhaps the most important element in the "loop." It is in this element that corruption derived from human inconsistencies is most likely to take place. *Orientation* should be purely objective, but can easily succumb to the subjective. Past experience in particular can influence *Orientation,* especially when considering previous successes or failures. Success seeks repetition, thus creating a dangerous tendency to fall into a predictable pattern of behavior not necessarily dictated by the *Observations* made. Likewise, defeat can retard the ability to consider options which, even if they have failed in the past, might very well be the keys to success in the current condition. There is a distinct need for a high level of self-awareness during this phase of the "loop."

The third element, *Deciding,* represents the process of selecting a given course of action from those that emerge from the first two elements of the "loop." Boyd described *Deciding* as "A complex process of analysis and synthesis before selecting a course of action. . . . We assess a variety of competing, independent channels of information from a variety of domains to cope with the particular circumstance which confronts us."

The ideal situation would exist if one could replicate Boyd's finite list of aerial maneuvers possible during the course of air-to-air combat. If such intimacy cannot be assured, then the next best position to be in is that in which one exhibits enough familiarity with a given set of circumstances to be comfortable when conducting any assessment leading to the necessity of making a decision in a timely fashion.

The fourth and final element, *Action,* is perhaps the most difficult to implement, since it involves the process of doing that which has been decided upon, and often involves forces that require additional prodding and/or persuasion before they act. Of course, once an *Action* has been taken, the OODA-Loop begins again, with the decider reorienting in relation to the problem, this time incorporating all of the new factors that might have emerged in the most recent cycling of the OODA-Loop. This is an ever-repeating process, which continues until the opponent is defeated.

The ideal application of the OODA-Loop takes place simultaneously at multiple levels. In upcoming chapters we will discuss strategic, operational, and tactical thinking, how the three are different, and how they interrelate. While it is important to separate these three "planes" of thinking when assessing each individually, one must always remember that the three take place simultaneously and feed off each other; and each individually develops, based upon how the others are behaving. This is a very dynamic environment, whether we are talking about modern warfare or organizing a field trip of retirees to Atlantic City. "Friction" is involved in each scenario, and any organization that can find and adopt the means to reduce its "friction" will in the end have the means to assure success.

The OODA-Loop is a process that provides systematic lubrication for the friction of conflict. Keep in mind that when engaged in conflict, there is a dynamic interplay between the opposing forces. Newton's three laws of motion are very applicable here. The first law—"Every object in a state of uniform motion tends to remain in that state of motion unless an external force is applied to it,"—reinforces the notion that doing nothing minimizes friction. Doing little creates less friction than doing much. The second law—"The relationship between an object's mass m, its acceleration a, and the applied force F is $F = ma$, or *F*orce equals *M*ass times *A*cceleration"—simply proves the point that to achieve motion, energy is expended, creating friction. The third law—"For every action there is an equal and opposite reaction,"—points out that nothing happens in isolation. Simply standing still creates friction, as the force of gravity pushes you to the earth, and the earth pushes back. When you decide to move, there will be friction created as forces push back against you. Never forget that this law applies to your opponent as well. The sooner you can get moving, the sooner you can reduce your accumulation of friction. The more you force your opponent to react to your initiative, the more friction is accumulated for your opponent.

Decision making is about achieving motion. It is about creating the conditions under which movement can take place. Motion is a process that inherently creates friction. Understand this: it is better to begin a conflict already in motion than to be standing still. If one is in motion, the amount of force required to achieve a change in direction (assuming one maintains a forward momentum) is less than if one begins from a full stop. *Action* is better than *Reaction,* because *Action* produces less friction than *Reaction* does. As such, if you can gain the initiative on an opponent, and enter into a cycle where you act and the opponent reacts, the laws of motion dictate there will be an accumulation of friction on the part of your opponent, which will lead to a inevitable spiral of defeat as you tighten your decision-making cycle, and your opponent widens his.

Master the OODA-Loop, and you will master conflict. This is the gift John Boyd gave us all. Progressives would do well to assimilate the OODA-Loop into their way of doing business.

You can be rest assured that your opponents are.

5

Intelligence Preparation of the Battlefield

The wicked are always surprised to find that the good can be clever.
—Luc de Clapiers de Vauvenargues

* * *

Continuing with the premise that life is conflict, and that in particular we currently find ourselves in a situation in which a certain segment of society (the progressive movement) is engaged in ideological conflict with certain antisocial forces (the religious right, and so on), we now turn our attention to a more thorough study of how to proceed in the actual conduct of this struggle. We have come to understand that in conflict the side that favors maneuverability, whether it is the physical movement of resources or the fluidity of ideas, has the advantage over the side that retains a static posture. We also have recognized that the side that is able to ascertain a given situation, develop a plan, and execute it rapidly will invariably be able to achieve a superior position from which to maneuver.

The OODA-Loop provides a pattern of decision making that breaks down the required elements. But the OODA-Loop provides for a broad-brush approach toward decision making. The reality is that almost any given situation contains inherent complexities that make a simple "observe-orient-decide-act" cycle bog down if there isn't a systematic approach that further breaks down the OODA-Loop into a more manageable process. In the military today this systematic approach is known as "Intelligence Preparation of the Battlefield," or IPB.

The U.S. Military defines IPB as a "systematic approach to analyzing the enemy, the weather, and the terrain in a specific geographic area." I don't want to encourage progressives to engage the religious right in a decisive battle on a given piece of terrain; far from it. However, while the military speaks of geographic areas, in ideological warfare we need to think in terms of spheres of conflict that are not necessarily physical in nature (keep in mind Clausewitz's concepts of war and politics). Politicians do this when canvassing a given district. Pollsters do this as well when dissecting the beliefs and attitudes of certain segments of society.

Applying the IPB process enables one to selectively apply and maximize whatever defines one's strength at critical times and locations, wherever an ideological struggle is being waged. The process used by the military to best achieve this involves four distinct phases: Define the Battlefield Environment, Describe the Battlefield's Effects, Evaluate the Threat, and Determine Threat Courses of Action.

Many people who reject a military model when assessing how best to confront their ideological rivals do so because they cannot see past the literal definitions of many terms and concepts used by those who write military doctrine, policy, and procedure. The progressives need to see past the guns, bombs, and planes their mental imagery conjures up when thinking of conflict, and understand that maneuver applies to intellectual and moral conflict as well, summing up the foundation of ideological warfare.

Understanding the battlefield is critical when speaking of any conflict. The first two phases of the IBP process (Define the Battlefield Environment and Describe the Battlefield's Effects) address this issue. The military is concerned about the enemy it faces, and since it maneuvers on the ground and in the air, it is likewise concerned about the weather and terrain of the specific region in which it will be operating, since these factors directly impact its ability to maneuver. In ideological warfare, the "weather" could best be described as the ideals and beliefs held by those for whom the struggle is being waged.

Remembering that ideological warfare, as it is waged in a representative democracy such as America, is a numbers game, the battlefield becomes in effect the mass of people each side is trying to win over to their cause. Just as clear skies and sunny weather favor aggressive maneuvering from a classic military sense, operating in a community or location that is ideologically similar to your cause provides for a certain freedom of operation that would not be the case if you were trying to bring your message to those less inclined to agree with you.

As muddy roads, flooded rivers, and cloudy skies slow down an advance or impede maneuver in military conflict, so does a small support base, indifferent population, or active opposition impede political maneuver and advance in ideological warfare. Improved roads, bridges, and advanced technology can overcome the detrimental effects of weather. A key in ideological warfare is to identify the corresponding "bridges," "roads," and "advanced technology" to overcome identified obstacles in the political terrain on which one will be operating. These can equate to methods of electronic information transmission (e-mail, web pages, blogs, cell phones, faxes, television, radio, etc.), traditional human-to-human interface (town meetings, lectures, seminars, teach-ins, etc.), or a combination thereof.

It is important to understand how each means is already established in a given area before assigning a priority of use to it. It makes no sense to develop an e-mail-based information solution in an area where the Internet is not widely available. Likewise, building a system of communication around faxes and mailed flyers in an area where everyone is operating electronically is not only inefficient, but also costly.

Beyond the political/ideological, there is a physical element that needs to be addressed. What defines a given conflict region? Where are the critical points of social infrastructure that need to be factored in? What is the economy like? Where are people employed, doing what, and by whom? Are there churches, and if so, how many, and what role do they play in a given society? The same question applies to schools and other social groups, such as labor unions, clubs, and civic organizations, such as the police force and fire department. This all needs to be known and understood before the battle is initiated, so that the OODA-Loop can work as efficiently as possible. The side that best knows and understands the "battlefield" will be better positioned to make the right decisions.

In ideological conflict, the "enemy" must still be considered. Who are they, what do they represent, how do they function, and why do they believe in what they do? These are all questions that must be considered, because before one can formulate an effective response to an ideological opponent, one must first be aware of that which one is opposing. You cannot solve a problem until it has been defined. The third and fourth phases of the IPB process (Evaluate the Threat and Determine Threat Courses of Action) assist in this definition.

We have already discussed the importance of comprehending and accepting the reality that in ideological conflict there is in fact an enemy, or if one chooses a softer term of art, opponent. It is absolutely necessary to identify this opponent, and one must understand what the opponent stands for, how the opponent operates, what socioeconomic segment of society is attracted to the opponent's cause (and why)—and more. Such an understanding enables one to become familiar with what is euphemistically referred to as an opponent's "doctrine."

IPB in ideological conflict seeks to integrate the opponent's "doctrine"(perhaps better defined as known past operating practices) with the existing political environment and physical realities of a given region as they relate to the mission at hand. By doing this, you can be better placed to determine and evaluate the capabilities of your opponents, identify and assess their vulnerabilities, and predict their probable courses of action. If you can predict an opponent's action, then you can anticipate their response.

IPB as a process, if correctly pursued, enables the side that carries it out more effectively not only to improve the "observe-orient" phase of the OODA-Loop but also to empower those who carry out an effective IPB process to conduct their basic decision making more efficiently and effectively, and to decisively and aggressively act on those decisions, since as many "unknowns" as possible have been removed from the equation.

Of course, one doesn't want to lean too far forward when anticipating, because this can lead to an early commitment of resources and effort in a direction not reflected by reality. One still needs to take action based upon facts; IPB simply enables an opponent's possible course of action to be assessed, enabling responses to be formulated in advance, so that if the opponent does in fact behave per the predicted model, this fact can be identified and acted upon in a more expedient and efficient manner.

There are additional tools used in the IPB process. One used by the military is known as "event templating." In military-based IPB, an event template is a model against which enemy activity can be recorded and compared. Event templating represents a sequential projection of events that relate to space and time on a given battlefield, and indicates an enemy's ability to adopt a given course of action. Simply put, event templating enables one to take what is known about what an opponent is capable of doing, and compare it with what is actually being done. This assists in predicting what the opponent may do next. This will be discussed in the context of the work of the progressive movement in the final chapter of this book.

From an analytical standpoint, this is very important in determining what one's opponent is up to. By accurately tracking what an opponent is doing on the "battlefield," one will be able not only to more accurately predict what an opponent might do next but also identify occasions when an opponent deviates from the "norm" by noting when a given identified course of action deviates from what was predicted. Such a deviation could identify a change in tactics and/or strategy on the part of an opponent, or point out that a given "doctrinal" model being used might in fact be flawed. This allows you to make adjustments so that your event templating will be more accurate in the future.

There are additional tools that help in the conduct of effective event templating. One of these is what is termed in the IPB process as a "Named Area of Interest," or NAI. As the visualization of an opponent's capabilities and likely courses of action develops, certain critical factors will become apparent, both in terms of actual physical locations, or ideological viewpoints, or whatever factors are being measured. These designated areas or factors are critical because it is estimated that significant events and activities will either take place at the designated location(s), or about the identified issues. Such areas are designated as NAIs, and must be placed under observation and analysis. Given that the conduct of such observation and analysis is a resource-consuming task, the number and location of designated NAIs should be limited to the ability of an organization to do the job. Simply calling everything an NAI does no good; there must actually be an analytical process behind the designation of something as an NAI. If done properly, NAI designation and monitoring will lead to the development of data that is critical to understanding the area of conflict and the opponent.

NAIs can also be developed to support a decision-making process the military refers to as the Decision-Support Template, or DST. DSTs graphically represent the projected situation, and as a conflict unfolds the DST identifies where and when a decision should be made to initiate a specific activity or event. This is basic cause-effect analysis, in which one identifies specific criteria that must occur before one initiates a particular action. DSTs provide a tool that enables the criteria in question to be monitored in relationship to other events unfolding on the battlefield.

In the military, a DST could identify a specific geographical feature that, when reached by the enemy forces, triggers the release of a reaction force. In ideological conflict, a DST could track public opinion concerning a specific issue in a given region, triggering a release of resources or initiation of a particular aspect of a public relations campaign when certain thresholds are met. DSTs bring a discipline to the decision-making process, since they are part of an overall system that anticipates enemy actions and develops effective responses in a way that speeds up the decision-making process and makes it more efficient.

One needs to be careful not to overstate the importance of the IPB process and its assessment tools. These processes will not, in their own right, create and communicate a clear picture of the field of battle. The IPB process produces a lifeless depiction of a dynamic reality. The reality of mud can never be adequately depicted on a map or corresponding overlay, nor can the biting cold of a strong wind on a rainy night. Likewise, graphic portrayals of public opinion can never do justice to the emotion of a political rally, or the hope that burns in the heart of people supporting a cause they truly support. These are nonlinear factors that are difficult to chart, but are real nonetheless. The diagram on page 101 provides a conceptual schematic showing how an IPB support graphic can be used to support the waging of peace.

Clausewitz spoke of the importance of psychological factors in conflict. He rejected a geometric, linear approach to warfare, and pointed out that the human spirit and morale were much more decisive factors on the field of battle than formations and lines on a map. Fatigue, danger, decisiveness, boldness, determination, and audacity all impact conflict in a deep way that is difficult to quantify and virtually impossible to depict graphically. These psychological factors represent a reality that must be integrated into the overall intelligence preparation of a battle. The side that fails to do so will end up drawing lines on a map and filling out figures on a chart that are completely disconnected from the reality of human conflict.

It is essential that those who conduct an intelligence preparation of the battlefield be familiar with the realities of conflict. To anticipate the effects of mud on vehicles, it is best to first experience the reality of mud. To quantify the impact of a political rally or demonstration, it would be best to experience these events.

Decision making is a process, and there are methodologies and analytical tools that can assist in this process. IPB is one of these. But while conducting IPB is a recommended function of any staff or group engaged in the conduct of conflict, ideological or otherwise, it is important never to lose touch with one's "gut" feeling, especially if it is based upon past experience. Likewise, never forget to continuously gauge the "heart" of those who are waging conflict, both on your side and on the opponent's.

Numbers are important, but numbers tend to melt away into nothing when there is a collapse of morale. Track the quantifiable, but never forget the unquantifiable. Both contain the key to success in conflict.

6

Strategy, Operations, Tactics, and the Art of Campaigning

The perfection of Strategy would be to produce a decision without any serious fighting.

—B. H. Liddell Hart

* * *

When I first mentioned the notion of adapting military philosophies for use in the antiwar movement, I was surprised by how many people within the progressive movement jumped at the notion, usually emphasizing their enthusiasm with "We could definitely benefit from some serious strategy."

On many occasions, these same enthusiasts would then turn to me and ask, "So what should our strategy be?" I would attempt to answer the question by discussing the concept of an agreed-upon "sovereign core," center of gravity, political foundation, or some other term or terms that underscored the importance of having an agreed-upon single point of reference that all involved parties are working from as their motivator and basis of moral authority.

Eyes would glaze over, and invariably a hand would shoot up (or in many progressive-type gatherings, where social order is eschewed, a voice would simply shout out), and I would be told,

"We don't need to know this. We want to know how we can ______." (Fill in the blank, but don't be modest: the usual request always aimed high, and normally involved some aspect of "changing the world.")

In short, the progressives wanted to get straight into a tactical solution, closing with and destroying the enemy through firepower and maneuver, to borrow from my Marine Corps past, and forgo all the theory and process that come before. This, of course, is nothing more than a recipe for failure. As Sun Tzu noted, "Strategy without tactics is the slowest route to victory. Tactics without strategy is the noise before defeat."

I am somewhat sympathetic to the urgency of those who thirst for sound tactics. However, all of the discussions in this book will come to naught unless one can take theory and transform reality. Tactics represent the "execution" phase of any plan, where the rubber meets the road. But tactics in isolation accomplish nothing. This is why it is critical that we discuss the concepts of Strategy, Operations, and Tactics, and how to bring all three elements together in a synergistic fashion called "campaigning."

Most people think they know the difference between Strategy, Operations, and Tactics. After all, we are fully capable of opening and reading a dictionary. A simple examination in the Merriam-Webster's dictionary shows that the word "Strategy" has two principal meanings. (1): *the science and art of employing the political, economic, psychological, and military forces of a nation or group of nations to afford the maximum support to adopted policies in peace or war*; and (2): *the science and art of military command exercised to meet the enemy in combat under advantageous conditions.*

Likewise, looking up "Operation" reveals the following: (1): *performance of a practical work or of something involving the practical application of principles or processes;* and more specifically, (2): *a usually military action, mission, or maneuver including its planning and execution.*

Finally, a search for "Tactics" gives us the following: (1): *a device for accomplishing an end;* and (2): *a method of employing forces in combat.*

So there we have it: Science and Art (Strategy), Performance and Action (Operations), and Devices and Method (Tactics). Volumes have been written about all three words, what they mean, and how to apply them. Most of these works relate to concepts revolving around military conflict; some have applied these terms within the context of business. My goal here is not to replicate these works, but rather to help adapt and simplify these concepts within the framework of ideological conflict waged on the battlefield of civil society, and help facilitate the reader's ability to link the three concepts into a seamless, unified framework of action we call the "Campaign."

Strategic thinking is done on a number of levels, addressing a myriad of issues. This is the big-picture stuff, working on a level one nominally assigns to the overall boss or director of a program or project. Operational actions basically take the goals and objectives of strategic thinking and break them down into separate functional areas. This would be the work of a division head or project manager. Tactics are the basic building blocks of operations, the specific actions that get things done. Team leaders and section heads are usually affiliated with this level of work.

Using a firefighting analogy, a fire chief thinks strategically. During an emergency, his strategic vision is "put out the fire." He doesn't tell people how to do this. He just tells them to get it done (usually as safely as possible). The chief is not worried about what is happening on the fire scene, but what will be happening in the future: Is there enough water? Are there enough firefighters? Do the resources match the problem?

Beneath the fire chief is an operations officer, usually a junior chief or captain. He or she takes the strategic vision of "put out the fire" and breaks it down into distinct operational assignments: search and rescue (looking for victims), ventilation (releasing hot gas and smoke from the building), and fire suppression (putting water on the fire and extinguishing it). The operations staff runs the real-time aspects of the fire. They deal with the now. Their information is fed to the chief, so he or she can monitor and adjust strategic plans, but they themselves do not get involved in the long term.

Each operational assignment is then broken down into the specifics of accomplishing it. These are the tactics: search the fire floor, raise a ladder to the upper floors, cut a hole in the roof using a saw, pull a fire hose, make entry into the house, use a straight stream or fog pattern of water to put the fire out. This is the work of the firefighter and the lieutenant. The operations personnel do not tell the firefighters and lieutenants how to do their jobs, they simply give big-picture tasks—for instance, ventilating the house. The lieutenant decides how best to do this based upon the situation, and then accomplishes the task.

There are three distinct levels of conducting business at a fire scene, and when combined together and properly coordinated, they result in the fire being put out, which was the overall strategic direction to begin with. Mission accomplished. But it wouldn't happen unless everyone understood their role in the overall problem. Not everyone gets to be chief. And the chief has no business being the lieutenant.

My experience with progressives to date indicates that there are more people who want to be "chief," and that these "chiefs" not only want to devise the overall "strategy" of their organization but also want to be in the midst of the action as well, holding a banner in a demonstration, or passing out the leaflets, or doing some other activity that certifies their status as an "activist." While this inclination to do something is noble, it is inefficient and serves as a recipe for failure. There must be a distinct differentiation between those who devise and implement strategy and those who execute strategy in the form of tactics. We will discuss these distinctions more in the next chapter, but it is essential to understand the differences between the two before going on.

Some in the antiwar movement might find it difficult to put the theories and philosophies of military conflict into perspective when they consider their own personal circumstances. While I don't pretend to have insight into every aspect of the antiwar movement, I will say this: there is no single aspect of the antiwar movement that could not benefit from the direct application of the theory of war as espoused here.

I have had the opportunity to discuss this phenomenon with some very ideologically committed members of the progressive/antiwar/peace and justice collective. They all have their own pet projects, each one designed to save the world from itself, so it seems. A very popular cause at the moment is the so-called counter-recruitment movement, in which activists target the recruitment of high school juniors and seniors by military recruiters trying to fulfill a recruiting quota in order to keep the ranks of America's all-volunteer military full. The main point to be made here, when discussing the notion of utilizing the Art of War when seeking to wage peace, is that counter-recruitment is not a strategy. It is not even an operational aspect of a strategy. It is merely a tactic, a tool to be used as part of a larger goal and objective.

Unfortunately, many in the counter-recruitment community continue to view their efforts in a strategic light, as if opposing military recruiters is an end unto itself. Unless one can place counter-recruitment into a context, however, it is doomed to fail as a tactic. Counter-recruitment in and of itself is simply a distracter, a noisy precursor of the inevitable defeat of the antiwar movement. Likewise, a pro-Constitution strategy that lacks sound tactics is likewise nothing more than an illusion of substance, and in the end any organization that limits itself to its embrace without devising the specifics of its implementation will find itself defeated in the end.

The key question here, therefore, is whether or not counter-recruitment is a tactic that is ideologically consistent with a pro-Constitution movement. I believe that the answer is yes, but only if one adopts the esteemed British strategist B. H. Liddell Hart's concept of the "indirect approach." To launch a "frontal assault" on the sensibilities of the mainstream American public by announcing that your organization is opposed to military recruiters operating on the campuses of American high schools is simply a recipe for defeat. As Liddell Hart said, the direct assault "provokes a stubborn resistance, thus intensifying the difficulty of producing a change of outlook." The indirect approach, however, involves the conversion of ideas achieved by "unsuspected infiltration of a different idea or by an argument that turns the flank of instinctive opposition."

The concept of the indirect approach makes use of at least three key philosophical points of departure set forth by Sun Tzu in his *Art of War:*

1. All war is based on deception;
2. The supreme excellence is to subdue the armies of your enemy without fighting a battle; and
3. He will win who knows when to fight and when not to fight.

Counter-recruitment, as currently practiced, is the antithesis of the indirect approach. It is very much an in-your-face tactic designed to directly confront what is seen by many of its proponents as an undesirable action—the presence of military recruiters in American high schools. The problem is that there is a distinct gap between the strategic directions being embraced herein (that is, a pro-Constitution core value, which is inclusive of the need to defend these values, a need that brings with it implicit support of a means of defense, such as the armed forces)—and the tactic of counter-recruitment. The tactic of counter-recruitment, by seeking to undermine the military recruiters who help populate the armed forces sworn to uphold and defend the Constitution, flies in the face of the core value it is supposed to uphold.

What is lacking is a context for the tactic. There needs to be an operations-level linkage between the strategic goal of pro-Constitutionalism and the tactical objective of counter-recruitment, one that brings both into focus and harmony with one another. This is the true nature and value of operational art.

Starting off with an accepted core value of pro-Constitutionalism, a strategic objective of upholding and defending the Constitution against all enemies, foreign and domestic, can be adopted. As such, the notion of an armed force dedicated to defending the United States and its Constitution is one that can readily be embraced. Using the "firefighter benchmark" discussed in Chapter Two, it is easy to see how developing and maintaining a broad base of support among the American population for this ideal is something that can readily be accomplished from this strategic direction. But remember, maintaining a viable armed force is not the strategic direction; upholding the Constitution is. The maintenance of a viable armed force becomes an operational task in support of the strategic direction. As such, it is subordinate to the strategic direction. This is what the counter-recruitment movement must latch on to: an armed force that deviates from the strategic direction of upholding the Constitution is one that then needs to be opposed.

How do you support a cause by opposing it? This, of course, is what happens if you undertake a tactic of counter-recruitment while embracing an operational directive of supporting a viable armed force. The answer lies in pointing out that the tactic is subordinate to the operational directive. If the goal is supporting viable armed forces, the operative word becomes *viable*. Viability is defined by the strategic direction, upholding the Constitution.

An armed force that veers from this strategic direction therefore loses viability. Therefore, an important element of any counter-recruitment movement, emphasizing again the fact that such a movement is tactical in its scope, must be one that embraces viable armed forces while rejecting unviable ones. The lack of viability must be linked to a deviation away from the strategic direction.

In order to counter military recruitment, therefore, one must be able to demonstrate how military service, under certain circumstances, represents a deviation from defending the Constitution. This is a tall order, especially when considering the "firefighter benchmark" that needs to be applied when attempting to sway mainstream public opinion. The objective is not to attack military service per se, but rather to emphasize the present circumstances that make military service incompatible with the strategic direction of supporting the Constitution.

The definition of these circumstances will define the tactics to be employed in any counter-recruitment effort. The use of economic incentives to lure potential recruits into military service before they understand the reality of military life and responsibility can be highlighted as incompatible with the strategic direction, since false advertisement has always constituted fraud. Likewise, any sort of failure to maintain integrity by the military recruiter represents a circumstance which should be opposed. Just using these two examples, two operational objectives designed to support the strategic objective emerge: provide economic alternatives to military service and monitor the performance and related ethics of military recruiters.

When implementing these operational objectives, the tactics of counter-recruitment emerge: job fairs, workshops on the reality of military service hosted by veterans, parent-outreach programs, and so forth. The "firefighter benchmark" dictates that these tactics avoid confrontations that seem antimilitary. Indeed, in the spirit of the indirect approach, these tactics should be conducted in partnership with the military recruiters, not in opposition to them. When conducting job fairs, invite military recruiters so that the target audience (high-school-age youth) can make a more informed choice. When conducting workshops on the reality of military service, invite military recruiters so that they can participate in what will then be a more balanced debate and discussion. Parent-outreach programs will have greater impact if they are seen to be part of a balanced, inclusive approach, as opposed to a reactive exclusionary movement.

For those of you in the progressive movement who have, at this point in time, thrown up your hands in exasperation over the notion of working with military recruiters, you would do well to keep in mind the old military adage that the best course of action is one that encourages the enemy to do what they want to do. In the spirit of *Intelligence Preparation of the Battlefield* (see Chapter Five), having some insight into the recruiters' goals and objectives, especially quotas and recruit delivery dates, anything that impedes the military recruiters' ability to achieve their quotas of recruits will have a detrimental impact on the recruiters themselves. This is why the Department of Defense has imposed itself on such nonmilitary matters as No Child Left Behind, in which federal education dollars are linked with giving military recruiters access to students. This is why the Department of Defense has implemented force-protection measures that target antiwar and counter-recruitment groups.

Conflict is friction. Friction consumes resources. The Department of Defense has considerably more resources available to engage the counter-recruitment movement than vice-versa. The tactics employed by the counter-recruitment movement should not be designed in a way to increase the friction brought to bear on the counter-recruiters, but rather to increase the friction within the military recruitment cycle. The tactics employed should also minimize any friction between the counter-recruiters and the public at large, and increase the friction between the military recruiters and the public. The easiest way to do this is to put pressure on the military recruiters' ability to make quotas, thereby increasing the pressure brought to bear by the Department of Defense on the military recruiters. This makes it more likely that recruiters will engage in fraudulent activities, which represent a deviation from the strategic direction of upholding the Constitution.

The goal of the counter-recruitment movement should be to oppose fraudulent recruitment, not legitimate recruitment. I joined the Marine Corps out of a sense of duty. Counter-recruiters should encourage anyone who feels that military service is a legitimate expression of their duty to country to join the military. It is fraudulent recruitment that should be opposed. Carefully balancing strategic direction, operational objectives, and tactical implementation will give the counter-recruiters a more balanced, far-reaching, and viable platform from which to do their work.

The concept of Strategy, Operations, and Tactics as outlined in the counter-recruitment example can be applied in any aspect of the progressive/antiwar/peace and justice agenda. A disciplined approach must examine issues along a logical continuum that traces an issue from its ideological core that to its practical implementation. This linkage must also provide for a system of feedback, which measures whether a course of action is achieving the desired results, or whether circumstances have changed and require new benchmarks to be established and monitored.

If done properly, the logical continuum from strategy, through operations, and on to tactics will clearly define the specific details of each stage. Strategic direction is always derived from the core value or concept. Once defined, this strategic direction should be continually reassessed from the standpoint of ensuring that it remains true to the core values and concepts from which it was derived. To use the firefighter analogy, if the strategic direction is to put out the fire, then the fundamental concepts involved in accomplishing this task are to save lives, preserve property, and put out the fire. These become operational objectives. "Saving lives" dictates a whole host of issues, each of which dictates a specific tactical course of action. So do "preserving property" and "putting out the fire." Each tactical course of action must be further defined as to what constitutes success and how this success will be measured.

As each tactical course of action goes into effect, it must be continuously evaluated against this performance benchmark. If the specific data points being measured do not show progress, one must consider changing the tactic. If after changing tactics progress continues to be slow or stymied, one needs to take a step back and evaluate the operational objective. Have circumstances changed, concerning the operational objective, which indicate that the objective should be modified? If so, one must be careful to trace the new circumstance back to the strategic direction before redefining the objective. This will ensure continuity of purpose and ideal.

By working through the strategic-operational-tactical continuum in this manner, you will ensure that your strategy is not the slow route to victory and that your tactics are not simply the noise before defeat. The link between strategy and tactics is operations. All must be brought into harmony with one another, and in doing so one provides the materials to manufacture a blueprint for winning.

Except on the rarest of occasions, the strategic-operational-tactical continuum does not exist in isolation. Life is conflict, and conflict is rarely resolved in a single battle, but rather in a series of battles that are fought either in sequence, simultaneously, or both. Understanding and capturing the synergy created by multiple battles is the art of the campaign. For the progressive/antiwar/peace and justice collective, mastering the art of campaigning is essential if victory is to be achieved.

A single battle usually becomes a fight of attrition, from which the side with the greatest resources emerges victorious. A campaign brings maneuver into the equation, allowing a side with fewer resources to use feint, redirection, speed, and movement to pick a battle at a time and place of its choosing in which a temporary superiority in numbers can be achieved. If sequenced correctly, these battles can wear down a superior force over time until the side that initially started as the inferior in numbers emerges victorious.

A successful campaign requires strong continuity among strategy, operations, and tactics. It demands effective decision making, a mastery of the OODA-Loop, and a detailed knowledge of the opponent, oneself, and the terrain where the campaign is being waged. A campaign is the ultimate expression of the Art of War. One can, in the course of a campaign, lose most of the battles and still emerge victorious, if each battle was fought to achieve a specific purpose that set in motion forces that were identified and incorporated into the next battle, and so on, until culminating in the decisive event.

In a successful campaign, nothing is left to chance. Everything is carefully planned out with an eye toward cause-and-effect relationships, seeking to create predictable opportunities that are then rapidly exploited before the opponent has a chance to react. The ideal campaign would be one in which so much friction was created simply through maneuver that the opponent was worn out without a single battle ever being fought. Anyone can fight and win a single battle. Only someone who has mastered all aspects of the Art of War can fight and win a campaign.

Progressives would do well to embrace this concept. The progressive movement spends an inordinate amount of time, energy, and resources planning and fighting single "battles," incorrectly labeling these events "campaigns." A demonstration is a battle, and if conducted in isolation, will result in nothing more than a waste of time and resources. A demonstration is a tactic, and if not linked to a strategic direction through clearly defined operational objectives, it will simply result in the ineffective diffusion of energy. A campaign combines the strategic-operational-tactical continuum with decision making and intelligence preparation of the battlefield to create a synergistic process combining art and science, which we call the Art of War.

You cannot hope to fight and win a campaign without having mastered all of its component processes. B. H. Liddell Hart understood this all too well. He disparaged the old maxim, "If you wish for peace, prepare for war." Those who followed this maxim, he believed, were trapped in the mistakes of the past, doomed to repeat them over and over again, usually in a losing cause. He instead adapted the maxim: "If you want peace, understand war." This idea captured the spirit of intelligence and vision necessary to minimize conflict by understanding it, and making the appropriate adjustments to circumstances in a timely fashion so that conflict could be avoided or minimized. This is the true Art of War. The progressive movement, in its goal of waging campaigns of peace, must incorporate the Art of War, and in particular demonstrate mastery of the campaign, if it is to have any chance of victory.

7

Organization and Incident Command

He that cannot obey cannot command.
—Benjamin Franklin

* * *

I have participated in numerous seminars and discussions with the progressive movement in which issues relating to organization and leadership were discussed. While some of my colleagues were willing to discuss the need for a well-defined command structure, most voiced disapproval. "We operate along democratic lines," one participant told me. "Everyone has a legitimate voice that needs to be heard. We exclude no one."

This participant, and many others, is a proponent of horizontal organization, in which all are equal and all have an equal say. I refer to this sort of organizational structure as "flat line," and compare it to the readout on a heart monitor when a patient has died—a flat line. Any organization that organizes along the flat-line principle is almost always doomed to failure.

Rapid decision making, the key to success in any conflict, is not the product of consensus, but of good leadership and, even more important, good followership. My experience with many of the groups in the progressive movement is that they possess very few genuine leaders, and even fewer good followers. All members need to have a say, it seems, and everyone knows best. The end result is chaos.

It is no surprise then that progressives have made such little headway in broadening their base beyond those who seem to accept the flat-line organizational model as sufficient to the task. Flat-line organization is not leadership by the many, as some in the progressive movement proclaim. It is the antithesis of leadership. Those who embrace flat-line organizational principles cannot generate decisive leadership or produce a membership capable of following such leadership if and when it emerges. They represent little more than a mob, with all the benefits of mob rule.

What the progressive movement needs more than anything is the organizational equivalent of an external defibrillator, something that sends a shock through the entire mob and generates a linear deviation away from the flat-line model so disastrously embraced by its members. On a heart monitor this deviation appears as a triangular "blip," indicating life. If the progressive movement hopes to sustain anything close to resembling organizational "life" capable of fighting and winning an ideological conflict, it needs to reject the flat-line model of universal equality and accept the reality that in any organization there must be those who lead, and those who follow. And the reality, which is difficult for the social egalitarians who tend to populate the progressive movement to accept, is that in any organization designed for rapid decision making and execution of those decisions, more are destined to follow than to lead.

Who is to command? This is an eternal question, and in the competition of egos, it represents an almost insoluble problem. Ideally, leadership should be derived through some sort of meritocracy, in which relevant qualifications combine with personality to create what society has come to recognize as the prototypical "leader."

Leadership is not for the timid, nor is it suitable for those who are insufficiently skilled in the tasks one expects to be executed by one's subordinates. There are times when extraordinary circumstances produce extraordinary leaders. But to sit back and wait for such an event to occur is akin to organizational suicide. The best organizations "produce" leaders through a systematic process of preparation and evaluation. In order to succeed, progressives need to develop such a system, and ensure uniform compliance with whatever standards are agreed upon.

I'm a big believer in not reinventing the wheel, and in the case of progressives, a model of command exists that would be more than suitable for its needs. Known as the "Incident Command System," or ICS, this system has been adopted by the U.S. government as the organizational/management system that will be used by all emergency response agencies in the United States. The U.S. government's definition of "incident" is limited, but from the perspective of the progressive/antiwar/peace and justice collective, an 'incident' can include just about any aspect of its work, from a demonstration to fundraising, from organizing a meeting to coordinating Internet communications. If there is a problem that involves bringing people and/or organizations together in a unified, organized manner, ICS is the solution.

The Federal Emergency Management Agency, or FEMA, has been kind enough to provide basic ICS training online, free to anyone who signs up. The basic IS-100, Introduction to Incident Command System, can be accessed at the following web site: www.training.fema.gov/EMIWEB/is/is100.asp. Its follow-on course, IS-200, Incident Command for Single Resources or Initial Action Incidents, can be accessed at: www.training.fema.gov/EMIWeb/IS/is200.asp. Members of the progressive movement should not be put off by the labels used in ICS as taught by FEMA. Just remember that ICS is a proven management model based upon established business management principles, and has been proven over time in thousands of emergency responses across the United States.

The key thing to remember is that ICS meets the needs of any incident, whether large or small. When applied properly, ICS enables different organizations to meld effectively into a single entity focused on accomplishing a singular mission or goal. This, of course, is the answer many in the progressive movement claim to be looking for when lamenting the disparate composition of its many widespread and diverse components. Don't let the FEMA label fool you; ICS is ideal for the progressive movement. And think of the irony that exists in using ICS in support of the progressive movement's agenda, which in many cases has citizen groups facing off against government agencies from many different jurisdictions. I can guarantee that these governmental agencies will be using ICS to deal with whatever situation the progressive movement creates or is involved in. If the progressive movement can master ICS and apply it in its work more effectively, it will have taken a major initial step toward getting inside the opponent's decision-making cycle, the objective of Boyd's OODA-Loop.

Rather than repeat the ICS lesson plan here in this book, I encourage readers to access the FEMA web sites, and at a minimum read through the material. Concepts such as "span of control" should become familiar to all. There is a common management shortcoming that is especially prevalent in the progressive movement. The average person is capable of managing three to seven separate individuals or resources, with five being considered the ideal. I would submit that in the interest of reducing friction and speeding up the OODA-Loop, that for the progressive movement three would be an ideal "span of control" for its incidents.

Don't get trapped in the lexicon used by FEMA in describing ICS. The progressive movement is fully capable of creating its own alternative lexicon that will blend the management concepts in the FEMA ICS lesson plans with language/titles/labels more appropriate to its reality. What is important, however, is that in adopting/adapting ICS to meet its needs, the progressive movement develop a common lexicon so that when one group refers to a position or organizational structure, everyone knows what it is referring to. It does no good to speak of command, and then have groups confuse each other by creating a Babel of terms and definitions that have no relationship to one another. For each definition, there should be only one corresponding term or word. Keep it simple, and reduce friction. Reduce friction, and speed the process. Speed the process, and defeat the opponent by getting inside their decision-making cycle.

It is also important that the progressive movement learn the concepts of roles and responsibilities. There can only be one commander, one boss. Likewise, as functions are broken down into organizational entities, it is critical that everyone with a task should operate only within the framework of the assigned task. The quickest way to increase friction and slow down the process is for people to get involved in processes where they have no business. Do your job. Let others worry about doing their own jobs. If the system is working, there will be someone supervising the overall activity, making sure all tasks are being accomplished, and reassigning resources and responsibilities as required. If you don't have that assignment, do not take it upon yourself.

IS-100 provides the building blocks of incident command. IS-200 provides the concepts of command. In many ways, this will be the most difficult aspect for many in the progressive movement to buy into. IS-200 discusses the chain of command, which is the orderly line of authority within the ranks of an organization. Chain of command is inherently triangular in structure, with a single point at the top representing the commander, or boss. The "flatliners" out there will balk at this. Chain of command can never be horizontal, however. That is simply chaos. IS-200 explains in detail the principles of command and the structures of command designed to facilitate effective control. Again, the lexicon and some of the structure can be adapted to fit the specific needs of the progressive movement, so long as there is universal agreement on such adaptations.

But the underlying principles of command are carved in stone. There can only be one commander for a given situation. The rest are followers. Any attempt to operate with multiple commanders means that there are well-defined fractures in place that can be exploited, either by an opponent or human nature, to destroy the effectiveness of any organization so organized. If there is one lesson that the progressive movement needs to learn, this is it. Everything else involved in the waging of conflict revolves around this most basic principle: unity of command. There can only be one person in charge for any given problem.

As important as it is to have one commander, it is also important to have all of the followers operate as a single, effective team. One can impose all of the structure in the world on a group, but unless everyone involved has bought into operating as a team, this structure will collapse. In the world of wildland firefighting, where the concepts of Incident Command were born, the issue of effective "followership" has been addressed by seeking to create a common understanding among all team members about the basic human factors involved in a group dynamic. Special courses of instruction that emphasize individual and group responsibilities regarding situational awareness, communications, attitude and stress barriers, and decision making are provided to all new firefighters in order to strengthen basic teamwork principles. Students involved in this training leave with a better understanding of their responsibilities to address human performance issues so they can better integrate into a team operating in fluid, dynamic situations.

The National Wildfire Coordination Group, or NWCG, is the agency responsible for training wildland firefighters across the United States. It has created a basic course of instruction known as L-180, or Human Factors on the Fireline. This course can be adapted to create an activist equivalent, or anyone with a knowledge and understanding of group dynamics can put together a course of instruction. The important thing is to train people to be comfortable in their roles as members of a team, even if they have to subordinate some of their individuality.

Once personnel are trained to become effective followers, they are ready to be trained to become effective leaders. Again, the NWCG has created a course, L-280, From Followership to Leadership, which instructs students in leadership values and principles, transition challenges for new leaders (taking command, as opposed to simply being a member of a team), situational leadership (adapting leadership styles and techniques to different leadership challenges), maintaining team cohesion in the face of adversity, and ethical decision making. In addition to developing an understanding of fundamental leadership principles, students taking this course will assess their own individual traits as well as their personal motivations for becoming a leader. An important aspect of any good leader is the ability to subordinate personal gain for the good of the team. You may be the commander, but you are only as good as the team you lead. Those who seek leadership positions for personal glory only doom themselves and their team to failure.

Again, the progressive movement need not rely exclusively on firefighter-specific training programs in order to shape its collective membership into fighting shape, so to speak. But it will have to come up with some sort of unified training program that has the support of all involved. I recently participated in a couple of seminars on "The Art of War for the Antiwar," one in Rowe, Massachusetts, the other in Burlington, Vermont. One of the biggest problems faced early on in both cases was the difficulty in translating intent into action. The people participating in these seminars were very good at expounding concepts, and equally incapable of acting decisively on these concepts. The Marine Corps taught me that you fight only as well as you train, the extension of which is to train in peace as you want to fight in war. The progressive movement needs to implement a vibrant and relevant training program that prepares its members, both leaders and followers, for the rigors of conflict. Such a training program must be unified in nature, so that someone trained in California might readily integrate with a group trained in New York, and vice versa.

A key element in such training is unity, which brings with it uniformity of terms and definitions. The progressive movement would do well to create a "standards" organization, one that has widespread membership and acceptance. In the field of firefighting, this organization is known as the National Fire Protection Association, or NFPA. NFPA standards are the backbone of the fire service, and influence every aspect of how the fire service functions. The NFPA standards also create a system of uniformity throughout the fire service, so that the standards applicable to New York are the same standards applicable to California.

I could sit down and write "standards" that could be included in this volume, but this would be a waste of time. Just as no firefighter would dare to impose his or her individual concepts and perceptions on all other firefighters, no single member of the progressive movement should try to dictate similar concepts to the entire collective. Firefighters bring together a group of experts who collectively prepare the standards used in the firefighting service. The progressive movement could likewise come together and create something along the line of a National Concerned Citizens Activism Association, or NCCAA, which could in turn create structures and related standards that facilitate the creation of a nationwide movement able to more effectively utilize resources to achieve identified goals and objectives.

NCCAA standards could be used to define standards for a basic organizational position that one could call "Activist I" (just like in the firefighting service, where we refer to your basic firefighter as "Firefighter I"). Thus, anyone who wants to join an antiwar or peace and justice activist movement would need to meet the basic requirements set forth by such a standard. Given the concept of a core value ideally associated with the progressive movement of adherence to the Constitution of the United States of America, a standard that sets forth familiarity with the history, content, and intent of the Constitution would be a good place to start.

The NCCAA could create an online course (similar to that used by FEMA for ICS) that enables someone to read the Constitution and related supporting material and take a test, upon the successful completion of which a certificate is issued. Other "core skills" that could be incorporated into an "Activist I" standard could include completion of the FEMA IS-100 and IS-200 courses, again a task that could be completed online and for which certificates are issued. Presentation of these certificates to any organization that has agreed to comply with NCCAA standards could lead to the individual being classified as an "Activist I," and as such able to function at the most basic level within an organization within the progressive movement.

Other positions could be created, such as "Activist II" and "Activist III," which would represent passing more advanced training thresholds, such as incident command and more specialized skill sets associated with organized activism, including communications, logistics, and information processing. Task Books for each position past "Activist I" could be created, listing observable skills derived from specified training, skills that are to be evaluated by a competent authority, usually someone in the chain of command who has at a minimum attained the position being tested for.

Once a certain competency in "activism" has been attained, participants could seek to specialize in their qualifications. Exactly which skill sets would be conducive for such specialization status would be the purview of a NCCAA-like organization, but could include communications, transportation, logistics, personnel management and administration, food, information processing and analysis, and command. Standards for each position would need to be defined and developed, as would a system of training, testing, and evaluating compliance with meeting these standards.

Beyond the activist specializations, there is the question of developing leaders. Again, as has been pointed out when discussing the NWCG L-180 Human Factors course, before one can become a good leader, one must first be capable of being a good team member. This is why it is recommended that the first step in any leadership development program be to make a good team member and a competent follower.

It is also important that a leader possess certain technical skills. It is difficult to imagine someone trying to lead a team if the leader has no understanding of the issues involved. A fire chief cannot lead firefighters without having been a firefighter at one time and possessing a fundamental understanding of the problems involved with firefighting. In the same way, someone involved in a leadership position within the progressive/antiwar/peace and justice collective should have experienced the reality of operating as a member of a team involved in activism.

* * *

Beyond the basic principles of leader-follower and teamwork comes the organizational reality of making the team actually function.

An NCCAA-like organization would need to develop definitions and models for organizational structures by type and function. Examples of such organizational-typing could include the following.

Personnel Support Units: Basic "grunt" units, with twenty persons organized into three 6-person subteams, with a team leader and deputy team leader. Need pamphlets passed out? Mobilize a PSU. Need demonstration support? Mobilize a PSU. PSUs could become the infantry of the progressive movement. PSUs could further be categorized by sustainability and mobilization factors. For instance, a "Type I" PSU would be able to mobilize with a week's notice to deploy on its own for up to seven days within a 500-mile radius of its home location. A "Type II" PSU could deploy with a week's notice for a period of one week within a 500-mile radius, but would require transportation support. The type-classification could get as specific as is required. The important thing would be to create a uniform program of organization in which one can make certain assumptions based upon the organizational unit's type and classification. In this way, if one were to plan a demonstration lasting a week, and the number of demonstrators calculated to be needed was 200, then a request could be made for 10 "Type I" PSUs.

Incident Command Teams: These are trained command staffs, with a commander, logistics chief, operations chief, media chief, and all other staff functions built in. These teams could be deployed to support a given "incident" or event. ICTs could be type-classified based upon the size of an incident to be managed.

Communication Support Teams: There are teams of ten persons capable of providing cell phone/fax/Internet support for up to five supported units. Again, CSTs could be type-classified as required.

Transportation Support Teams: These teams are able to support a PSU with basic transportation requirements. Again, TSTs could be type-classified as required.

Food Support Teams: These teams are able to sustain a given number of PSUs with food and beverages for a specified deployment length.

* * *

Other organizational units could include Media Support Teams, Legal Support Teams, Medical Support Teams, Shelter Support Teams, Information Support Teams, Analytical Support Teams, or anything else one is able to come up with. The importance of specifying a team structure and mission is critical not only in planning a given incident but also in organizing the base of the progressive movement.

People have long been asking, "What can I do?" If the progressive movement could organize itself along the lines suggested here, then the answer is simple: fill out a "capabilities/offerings" sheet, submit it to your nearest activist organization, and find yourself put in contact with the nearest organizational entity that needs what you can bring to the table. You might be asked to join a PSU, or a TST, or any other organizational unit that is out there. Or if there are a number of you who want to work together, you could contact the NCCAA and request to be registered as a given organizational unit. The NCCAA would assist your team in getting the basic training required, and then work with your team to certify you as mission capable.

It is very hard for individuals to see how they can make a difference in isolation. By creating an NCCAA-like organization and putting in place a defined organizational structure, the progressive movement creates opportunities for more people to get involved. And by getting involved as part of an organized team structure, the new activists can multiply their effectiveness by reducing the friction and expense of activism. Looking back on the work of the progressive movement over the years, I have witnessed a tremendous duplication of effort, inefficient use of resources, and overall waste. Through better organization, the progressive movement will be able to streamline its activities to better identify what needs to be done, organize the resources needed to get the job done, and oversee the timely and efficient implementation of the task.

Just as an aerospace company does not rush off to build a fighter jet upon initial conception, the progressive movement should not rush off to build an organizational structure after initial discussion. The concepts provided here are just those: concepts. The specifics need to be developed that will dictate the particulars of any organization. A key tool for developing these specifics is the use of simulations or war gaming. An aerospace company would build a computer model of its aircraft design and run it through a number of simulations in order to better evaluate its design. Similarly, the progressive movement could develop simulations that test its theories, whether organizational or otherwise, before actually putting the ideas into practice.

Simulations can be as basic or as complicated as one likes. A good place to start when evaluating your own simulation needs is to look at past incidents in which you were involved and attempt to recreate one or more in simulation form. Assign different roles to personnel involved, and replay the incident over and over, identifying critical nodes and activities. Highlight what went right, as well as what went wrong. Make sure everyone involved is as honest as possible in the re-creation, so that no relevant detail is left out. Once the data has been captured, create organizational structures to deal with identified shortfalls or to reinforce identified successes. Simulate the existence of these structures, and feed them back into the scenario to evaluate how the presence of these new organizational structures could have had a positive impact on your mission goals and objectives.

If you are planning an activity such as a demonstration, it might help to "war game" it out ahead of time in order to anticipate your needs, as well as the reactions of your opponent. By anticipating requirements ahead of time, the progressive movement can better prepare for fulfilling its needs ahead of time, thereby reducing friction and speeding up decision making and offsetting out on a given course of action.

In the end, everything comes back down to the basic principles of the OODA-Loop: John Boyd was able to anticipate his opponent's possible responses to a given course of action, and immediately identify a particular course once it was decided upon, thereby coming up with a response that helped him maintain the advantage throughout the engagement. Simulations will not enable you to predict the activities of your opponent with 100 percent accuracy, but they will help you prepare in advance for as many contingencies as possible. Through this preparation one can better exploit the strength obtained through good leadership and effective organization.

Conclusion

ON WINNING

In War, there is no substitute for Victory.
—General Douglas MacArthur

* * *

Reading this book will not make you a "winner," just as it will not stop you from "losing." Reading this book will, however, give you tools to create the conditions of conflict conducive to your victory and your opponent's defeat. Victory does not simply happen; it is something that is produced through effort, sometimes extraordinary effort. Bear in mind that in conflict you are in almost all occasions confronting an opponent who is as determined to win as you should be. This opponent is looking for any sign of weakness on your part, and will be certain to exploit this weakness with as much decisiveness and ferocity as can be brought to bear. If you are not prepared to confront such an opponent, then don't enter the field of battle. Conflict is not for the faint of heart. In conflict you must be prepared to knock your opponent down, and then, instead of offering a helping hand, hold your opponent down with the heel of your foot while you plunge a bayonet into his or her heart. You can be assured that your opponent would do the same to you.

The bayonet, of course, is metaphorical. In this book we are discussing ideological conflict, not actual physical warfare. But in framing a clash of ideas as conflict, you must be prepared to destroy your opponents' idea and their ability to sustain and spread their idea. You must fight with all the vigor of a marine who seeks to destroy the life of those he faces on the field of battle. Sun Tzu speaks of ferocity in combat. People who wage peace must be ferocious in their determination to prevail. Conflict cannot be entered into halfheartedly. This is the battle for America's future we are talking about. This is as serious as it is real. There is no second place in this struggle, only victory. And victory will come only to those who prepare themselves to win.

For those who were looking for a blueprint, a step-by-step "how to" manual for waging conflict, a "playbook" that charts a path to victory, you are bound to be disappointed in this book and you have demonstrated through your mind-set that you are in fact preprogrammed for defeat. But if you recognize that the path to victory lies at the other end of a dense forest, and that this book provides you with an ax and directions on how to fell a tree, then you are well on your way toward prevailing in conflict.

The steps toward winning set out in this book are simple:

1. Prepare yourself for conflict by recognizing the reality of conflict.
2. Establish a solid foundation from which to wage conflict by identifying your center of gravity.
3. Understand that conflict is fluid, that proactive movement trumps reactive movement, and that all movement generates friction. The side that generates less friction usually prevails.
4. Decision making is a key to reducing friction. Being able to make decisions faster than your opponent is

therefore a key to victory. The OODA-Loop must be mastered.

5. Know your enemy as well as you know yourself. Know the terrain upon which a battle will be fought. Anticipate your opponents' actions through a thorough understanding of how they fight. Make your enemy do what they are already inclined to do; by anticipating this, you will be able to set a trap that facilitates their destruction.
6. Strategy and Tactics in isolation are recipes for disaster. Strategy and Tactics linked through Operational thinking provide the tools for winning.
7. Conflict is more than a single battle. Be prepared to wage a series of battles in order to emerge victorious. Link these battles together in a synergistic fashion, creating a campaign that highlights your strengths while exploiting the weaknesses of your enemy.
8. Be decisive in victory. Dominate and destroy your enemy.

Winning, like losing, is learned behavior. In the military, commanders often seek to conduct smaller, "proving" battles or raids, which not only exercise their troops, but also condition them to win. Conflict is very much psychological. Moral defeat is far more devastating than physical defeat. By learning to win, you are teaching your opponent to lose. Develop the skills needed for achieving victory by conducting realistic simulations of conflict, in which all aspects of the coming battle are "war gamed" out in advance.

This kind of anticipatory behavior has long been the bane of the progressive/antiwar/peace and justice collective. There have been occasions on which the antiwar movement stumbled into a strategic opportunity, and then squandered it through the inability to predict the next step and effectively prepare for it. The most dramatic example of this was the standoff outside Crawford, Texas, in the summer of 2005, when Cindy Sheehan bravely confronted President Bush over the death of her son in Iraq. This was a courageous and brilliant move on her part, one made even more so by an accident of history: no major competing events diverted media attention away from her cause.

For weeks Cindy Sheehan was able to capture the imagination and sympathy of America as the president made blunder after blunder in responding to her actions. "Camp Casey" became a center of gravity, so to speak, for the antiwar movement. And then it ended. The battle was won, but there was no campaign being waged. There was no systematic means of following up on the considerable achievement that was "Camp Casey." The energy and momentum that was created by Cindy Sheehan's action was soon frittered away. At the time of this writing, more than 3,000 American sons and daughters, just like Casey, have perished in Iraq. Tens of thousands more have been wounded and maimed. *Hundreds of thousands* of Iraqis have suffered a similar fate, with no end in sight. A Democratically-controlled Congress, allegedly empowered by the antiwar sentiment of the American people, is preparing to support a "surge" of American troops into Iraq, actually increasing the friction that generates dead and wounded Americans and Iraqis. "Camp Casey," a victorious battle in the cause of peace, will go down in history as part of a losing campaign unless something is done to change the organizational dynamic of the progressive movement and its peace and justice activists.

The progressive movement would do well to recapture the entire "Camp Casey" experience, documenting every move made by both sides and using it as a case study from which important lessons can be garnered and applied to future efforts. Create a conflict simulation, so to speak, pitting the progressive movement against the pro-war movement, and use the real experiences garnered from "Camp Casey" as the foundation. Refight "Camp Casey" over and over again, using the theories and models of conflict put forward in this volume. Examine "centers of gravity." What made each side tick? Evaluate decision making on both sides, both in isolation and in relation to each other. Look at the problems associated not only with the physical support of "Camp Casey" (the movement of people, food, shelter, funds, etc.) but also the movement of ideas (the media, vision projection, who was saying what and when, and were these messages being coordinated, and, if so, how).

Plotting out these different factors in a coherent and unified manner makes it possible to begin visualizing the ideological battlefield. Once this battlefield is defined, go back and reread the chapter on "Intelligence Preparation of the Battlefield." Take each factor that has been developed, and project it onto this battlefield. Plot the movement of personnel together with the accumulation of funding requirements. Identify where the needs for funding, food, and other support were first identified, and how they were actualized. See what elements of this process were predictable in advance, and how organizational structures could be developed to help facilitate the early manifestation of these processes. Suddenly the foreign concepts of "event templating," "named areas of interest (NAI)," "decision support template (DST)," and others come to life. "Camp Casey" didn't just happen. It represented a confluence of ideas and personalities, triggered by Cindy Sheehan's courageous stance. It was the quintessential expression of "politics," and hence "war" or "conflict." It has elements that are identifiable, definable, and thus discernable. It should be studied and analyzed by the progressive movement with the same attention to detail and search for meaning with which the great battles of history have been studied by the military.

"Camp Casey," the massive peace demonstrations of 2002–2003, and every other aspect of the work conducted by the progressive movement needs to be put through a detailed after-action critique. Important lessons can be developed through this process. Once these lessons are identified, conduct simulations of these events should be carried out, this time applying the Art of War concepts found in this book. See what could have been done differently, when this could have been done, and why it should have been done. Examine not only the actions of the progressive movement but also those of the enemy. Why did the enemy do what it did? When were decisions made by the enemy? What influenced these decisions? How might the progressive movement better exploit enemy weaknesses? How could the progressive movement minimize the enemy's strengths? How could the progressive movement have achieved overall victory in the campaign to stop the war in Iraq and bring the troops home? Are there any lessons that can be learned and applied to the upcoming possibility of conflict with Iran? Winning requires hard work and sacrifice. It will not come easily, and it will not come without a price to be paid.

Allies are very important in any conflict. Early on in this book we discussed expanding the base of support among the American people. These aren't allies; these are supporters. Supporters are permanent and allies are temporary. Each conflict, each battle, must be evaluated from the standpoint of who will be affected by what. Seek out those who would be naturally sympathetic to your cause, and nullify those who are inclined to be in sympathy with your opponent.

Because the ideological conflict being waged in America is being carried out on a global battlefield, those who wage peace should not limit themselves to simply fighting battles and campaigns in America. There is a global antiwar/peace and justice movement out there that the American progressive movement should tap into. I have spent a great deal of time over the past few years traveling around the world and meeting with some fantastic antiwar/peace and justice movements and organizations. Whether it was working with French, Italian, British, Danish, and German supporters of peace and justice to highlight the fallacy of President Bush's hyped claims regarding Iraqi WMD in the summer/fall of 2002, or cooperating with Japanese peace workers in an effort to influence the Japanese Parliament prior to the initiation of conflict with Iraq in February 2003, assisting Irish antiwar activists as they fought criminal charges brought on by their opposition to the war in Iraq, or working with British parliamentarians to pressure Prime Minister Tony Blair over the so-called dodgy dossier in 2004, to touring Australia with antiwar activists in 2005 in an effort to hold Prime Minister John Howard to account for his support for America's war in Iraq, or traveling to Iran to highlight the misrepresentation of facts concerning Iran's nuclear programs by the United States in 2006, I have come to know and understand and sympathize with the millions of fellow citizens of this planet who yearn for peaceful coexistence in a world populated with the nations united in the cause of justice and prosperity.

Many of these movements suffer from the same problems and issues that plague their American counterparts. Many of these movements have ideas and procedures that can benefit the work of their colleagues around the world.

Of course, the overseas peace and justice movements have organizational roots that go deeper in history than their counterparts here in the United States. In America the progressive movement seems to possess a perpetual "hangover" stemming from the "free love" attitude of the 1960s. Our overseas counterparts have stronger structural components in their organizations due to their strong labor roots, which bring with them the socialist rigor of Marxist-Leninist doctrine, which possessed a quasi-militaristic foundation from an organizational standpoint. I am in no way suggesting that the progressive movement in America should embrace Marxist-Leninist ideology or practices. Just the same, we all would do well to recognize the similarity in nature and cause with the working class of Europe, which responded to the teachings of these socialist philosophers, and the majority of Americans today, whether they be poor or middle class, and whatever their needs and wants as a social movement in waiting may be. American trade unions have long embraced organizational structure and hierarchy when seeking to organize the masses. The progressive movement in America would do well to remember that. There is a reason progressive movements abroad do better than the American progressive movement when it comes to influencing politics and policy: movements abroad are much better organized.

The American progressive movement has not always been this devoid of leadership and structure. One only need to study the life and achievements of Saul Alinsky, a Chicago-based former criminologist who revolutionized the grassroots movements of the 1950s and 1960s into genuine political movements possessing real political power. Through his Industrial Activities Foundation (IAF), Alinsky was able to help working class communities organize into community councils, which were able to provide basic services to those in need, and then turn the masses attracted to these services into real political power. Saul Alinsky believed in organization, complete with a hierarchy of leadership. This is what made him effective, and it is what ultimately brought him down. The progressive movement of today seems to embrace the politics of the "new left" that emerged in the 1960s (in particular that element led by Tom Hayden and others), in which "participatory democracy" as defined by Hayden in his Port Huron statement of 1962 trumped Alinsky's "citizen participation."

"As a social system," Hayden and his fellow students wrote, "we seek the establishment of a democracy of individual participation, governed by two central aims: that the individual share in those social decisions determining the quality and direction of his life; that society be organized to encourage independence in men and provide the media for their common participation." Hayden went on:

> In a participatory democracy, the political life would be based in several root principles:
>
> - that decision-making of basic social consequence be carried on by public groupings;
> - that politics be seen positively, as the art of collectively creating an acceptable pattern of social relations;
> - that politics has the function of bringing people out of isolation and into community, thus being a necessary, though not sufficient, means of finding meaning in personal life;
> - that the political order should serve to clarify problems in a way instrumental to their solution; it should provide outlets for the expression of personal grievance and aspiration; opposing views should be organized so as to illuminate choices and facilitate the attainment of goals; channels should be commonly available to relate men to knowledge and to power so that private problems—from bad recreation facilities to personal alienation—are formulated as general issues.

The Tom Hayden of this period was a "flatliner," someone who embraced the horizontal organizational structures popular with the American progressive movement of today. Saul Alinsky was someone who embraced strong leadership, organizational structure, and centralized decision making. The politics of the New Left have left the American progressives (and indeed many of America's underclass) feeling powerless and helpless. This is the political end result of feel-good "participatory democracy," in which one waits in hope for the collective to deliver on the false promise of the brotherhood of mankind.

Saul Alinsky preached "citizen participation," a totally different concept, which had those in need organizing and taking care of their needs themselves. He wasn't dismissive of democratic processes, recognizing that the desire of people to become involved in the decision-making process was the fundamental reason behind organizing. He simply recognized the importance of bringing structure and organization together with unity of purpose and command in order to empower the people to successfully confront the systematic advantages enjoyed by the privileged class in a capitalistic society, to help inspire them to actively change their own circumstances.*

The "participatory politics" embraced by the Hayden-influenced New Left–inspired progressives of today have, as predicted by Alinsky, created the conditions in which the poorer classes of America have been lost to more right-wing politics, which preyed upon unfulfilled needs with false promises of economic benefits "trickling down" from capitalistic largess. The progressive movement of today is engaged in a conflict with its ideological opponents to win these Americans back. This cannot be done by calling for revolutionary change in America, as some on the left today propose. What change that will come must come from within the system, Alinsky-style, not in changing the system, Hayden-style. Alinsky wanted a movement with staying power, as opposed to a movement of instant power. This is perhaps the biggest lesson the progressive movement of today could take away from the organizational theories of Saul Alinsky: Staying Power. Never forget the concept of Constitutional core value, and its inherent attraction to

* I am indebted to David Sirota's essay discussing Sandford D. Horwitt's biography of Saul Alinsky posted on the Huffington Post.

the American masses. This is the ideological battlefield on which the conflict for the future of America is being waged.

The proponents of the need for systematic "change" in America today who populate the progressive movement often speak the language of "revolution," and quote revolutionaries, like Ernesto Che Guevara. Some even speak of the need for "guerrilla politics," alluding to the peoples-based "guerilla war" Che called for. "Why does the guerrilla fighter fight?" Che asked. "We must come to the inevitable conclusion that the guerrilla fighter is a social reformer, that he takes up arms responding to the angry protest of the people against their oppressors, and that he fights in order to change the social system that keeps all his unarmed brothers in ignominy and misery." This, of course, is a quote many in the "New Left" find attractive.

But they would do well to read Che in his entirety. "Where a government has come into power through some form of popular vote, fraudulent or not, and maintains at least an appearance of constitutional legality, the guerrilla outbreak cannot be promoted, since the possibilities of peaceful struggle have not yet been exhausted." America is a nation that maintains more than the simple appearance of constitutional legality. We are a nation born of its Constitution, and as such can be nurtured only through this very same Constitution. Given how far off course we as a nation have collectively strayed from the ideals and values in the Constitution, we must find it in ourselves to collectively navigate our way back to the course directed by the Constitution. We will find that Saul Alinsky's "citizen participation" is by far a better model to follow than Hayden's "participation democracy." Implicit in Alinsky's thinking is the concept of the citizen, a being born from commonality of purpose as set forth by a central set of values and vision such as exists in the Constitution. As long as we hold true to these values, the possibilities for peaceful struggle, as Che stated, will never be exhausted.

The American progressive movement would do well to seek to expand its base of support among these international fellow travelers on the path toward peace. As I have pointed out, the international progressives already possess an impressive organizational structure and capabilities. What is lacking is a common center of gravity, a unifying thematic, Che Guevera's proverbial system of "constitutional legality" recognizable by all. While the United States Constitution may not resonate among our non-American colleagues, we in America should look to the Constitution for guidance to identify a center of gravity that would bind everyone in the world to the goal of bringing an end to the war in Iraq, preventing a needless war with Iran, and terminating conflict derived from the ideologies of hate and greed. Article VI of the United States Constitution provides the key to finding such a core value: "This Constitution, and the Laws of the United States which shall be made in Pursuance thereof; and all Treaties made, or which shall be made, under the Authority of the United States, shall be the supreme Law of the Land; and the Judges in every State shall be bound thereby, any Thing in the Constitution or Laws of any State to the Contrary notwithstanding."

The United States, like most nations in the world today, has signed the Charter of the United Nations, a document that has been ratified by the United States Congress and thus, in accordance with the U.S. Constitution, becomes "the supreme Law of the Land." Appendix B contains the United Nations Charter in its entirety. As is the case with the U.S. Constitution, this document should be read and understood by all in American progressive movement, who should then encourage all Americans to read it as well, since it is by extension part of the very Constitution we are bound as citizens to uphold and defend. And we should encourage those in the global antiwar/peace and justice movement to study the Art of War as well, so that there can be a worldwide waging of peace that might prevail over the forces of those who pursue war, death, and destruction. Create a movement of global citizens who can work for peace and justice, instead of being pawns used by others for purposes antithetical to the global progressive cause.

And so we come full circle, from center of gravity to center of gravity. The cause is just, the situation grave, and the need for resolve in the face of adversity real. If you have taken the time to read this book from cover to cover, then there is no doubt in my mind you are committed to the path of waging peace using the tools provided by the Art of War until victory is achieved. On behalf of all those who will benefit from the fruits of your labor, those alive today and those yet to be born, I thank you. Now get out there and get the job done.

Intelligence Preparation of the Battlefield (IPB) Support Graphic Template
(Notional Demonstration Activity)

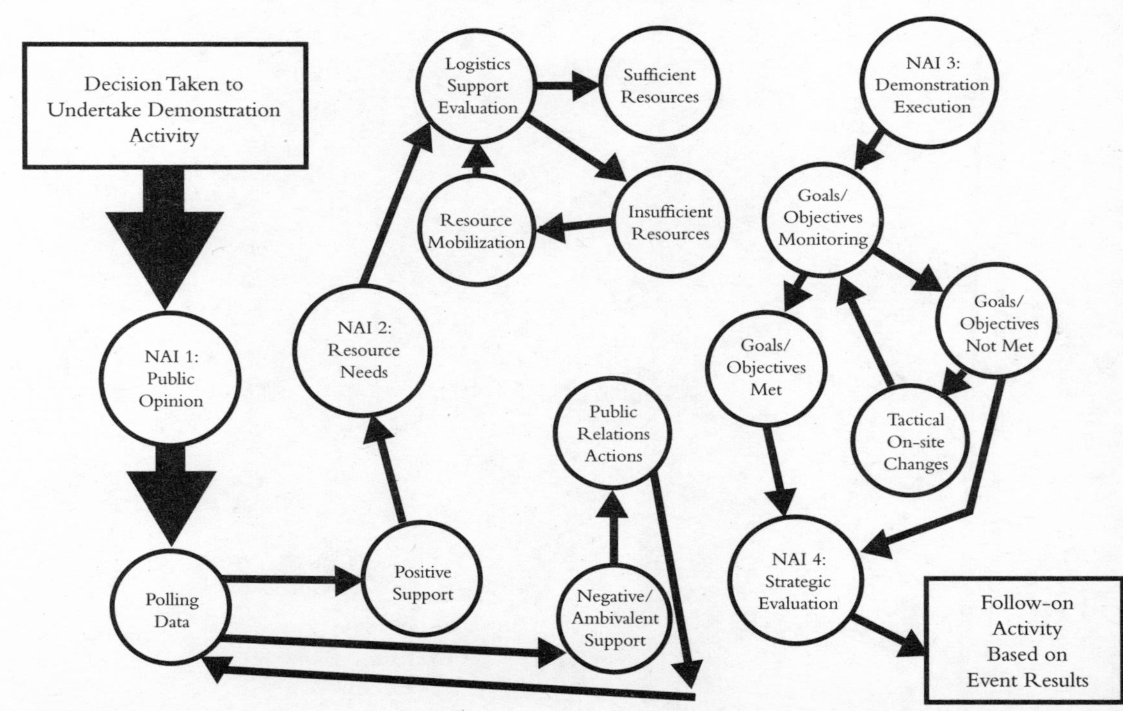

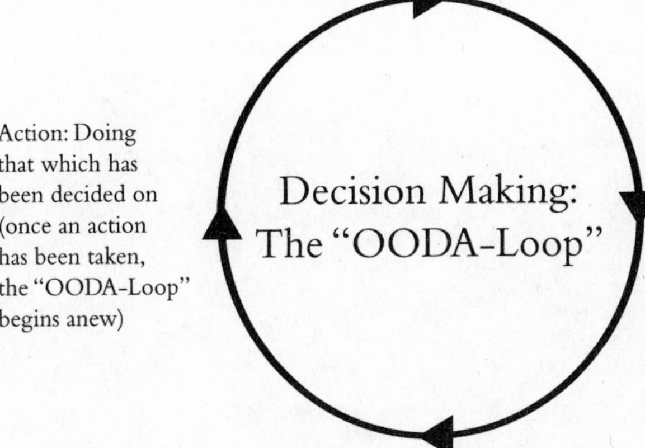
Observation: Seeing, sensing and comprehending one's own environment, as well as that of one's opponent
Orientation: Objective positioning of one's self in relation to observations made
Deciding: The selection of a given course of action derived from observations made and subsequent orientation of one's self
Action: Doing that which has been decided on (once an action has been taken, the "OODA-Loop" begins anew)
Decision Making: The "OODA-Loop"

Appendix A

THE CONSTITUTION OF THE UNITED STATES OF AMERICA

Preamble

We the People of the United States, in Order to form a more perfect Union, establish Justice, insure domestic Tranquility, provide for the common defence, promote the general Welfare, and secure the Blessings of Liberty to ourselves and our Posterity, do ordain and establish this Constitution for the United States of America.

Article I. The Legislative Branch

Section 1. The Legislature

All legislative Powers herein granted shall be vested in a Congress of the United States, which shall consist of a Senate and House of Representatives.

Section 2. The House

The House of Representatives shall be composed of Members chosen every second Year by the People of the several States, and the Electors in each State shall have the Qualifications requisite for Electors of the most numerous Branch of the State Legislature.

No Person shall be a Representative who shall not have attained to the Age of twenty five Years, and been seven Years a Citizen of the United

States, and who shall not, when elected, be an Inhabitant of that State in which he shall be chosen.

Representatives and direct Taxes shall be apportioned among the several States which may be included within this Union, according to their respective Numbers, which shall be determined by adding to the whole Number of free Persons, including those bound to Service for a Term of Years, and excluding Indians not taxed, three fifths of all other Persons. The actual Enumeration shall be made within three Years after the first Meeting of the Congress of the United States, and within every subsequent Term of ten Years, in such Manner as they shall by Law direct. The Number of Representatives shall not exceed one for every thirty Thousand, but each State shall have at Least one Representative; and until such enumeration shall be made, the State of New Hampshire shall be entitled to chuse three, Massachusetts eight, Rhode Island and Providence Plantations one, Connecticut five, New York six, New Jersey four, Pennsylvania eight, Delaware one, Maryland six, Virginia ten, North Carolina five, South Carolina five, and Georgia three.

When vacancies happen in the Representation from any State, the Executive Authority thereof shall issue Writs of Election to fill such Vacancies.

The House of Representatives shall choose their Speaker and other Officers; and shall have the sole Power of Impeachment.

Section 3. The Senate

The Senate of the United States shall be composed of two Senators from each State, chosen by the Legislature thereof for six Years; and each Senator shall have one Vote.

Immediately after they shall be assembled in Consequence of the first Election, they shall be divided as equally as may be into three Classes. The Seats of the Senators of the first Class shall be vacated at the Expiration of the second Year, of the second Class at the Expiration of the fourth Year, and of the third Class at the Expiration of the sixth Year, so that one third may be chosen every second Year; and if Vacancies happen by Resignation, or otherwise, during the Recess of the Legislature of any

State, the Executive thereof may make temporary Appointments until the next Meeting of the Legislature, which shall then fill such Vacancies.

No person shall be a Senator who shall not have attained to the Age of thirty Years, and been nine Years a Citizen of the United States, and who shall not, when elected, be an Inhabitant of that State for which he shall be chosen.

The Vice President of the United States shall be President of the Senate, but shall have no Vote, unless they be equally divided.

The Senate shall choose their other Officers, and also a President pro tempore, in the absence of the Vice President, or when he shall exercise the Office of President of the United States.

The Senate shall have the sole Power to try all Impeachments. When sitting for that Purpose, they shall be on Oath or Affirmation. When the President of the United States is tried, the Chief Justice shall preside: And no Person shall be convicted without the Concurrence of two thirds of the Members present.

Judgment in Cases of Impeachment shall not extend further than to removal from Office, and disqualification to hold and enjoy any Office of honor, Trust or Profit under the United States: but the Party convicted shall nevertheless be liable and subject to Indictment, Trial, Judgment and Punishment, according to Law.

Section 4. Elections, Meetings

The Times, Places and Manner of holding Elections for Senators and Representatives, shall be prescribed in each State by the Legislature thereof; but the Congress may at any time by Law make or alter such Regulations, except as to the Places of chusing Senators.

The Congress shall assemble at least once in every Year, and such Meeting shall be on the first Monday in December, unless they shall by Law appoint a different Day.

Section 5. Membership, Rules, Journals, Adjournment

Each House shall be the Judge of the Elections, Returns and Qualifications of its own Members, and a Majority of each shall constitute a Quorum to do Business; but a smaller number may adjourn from day to day, and may be authorized to compel the Attendance of absent Members, in such Manner, and under such Penalties as each House may provide.

Each House may determine the Rules of its Proceedings, punish its Members for disorderly Behavior, and, with the Concurrence of two-thirds, expel a Member.

Each House shall keep a Journal of its Proceedings, and from time to time publish the same, excepting such Parts as may in their Judgment require Secrecy; and the Yeas and Nays of the Members of either House on any question shall, at the Desire of one fifth of those Present, be entered on the Journal.

Neither House, during the Session of Congress, shall, without the Consent of the other, adjourn for more than three days, nor to any other Place than that in which the two Houses shall be sitting.

Section 6. Compensation

The Senators and Representatives shall receive a Compensation for their Services, to be ascertained by Law, and paid out of the Treasury of the United States. They shall in all Cases, except Treason, Felony and Breach of the Peace, be privileged from Arrest during their Attendance at the Session of their respective Houses, and in going to and returning from the same; and for any Speech or Debate in either House, they shall not be questioned in any other Place.

No Senator or Representative shall, during the Time for which he was elected, be appointed to any civil Office under the Authority of the United States which shall have been created, or the Emoluments whereof shall have been increased during such time; and no Person holding any Office under the United States, shall be a Member of either House during his Continuance in Office.

Section 7. Revenue Bills, Legislative Process, Presidential Veto

All bills for raising Revenue shall originate in the House of Representatives; but the Senate may propose or concur with Amendments as on other Bills.

Every Bill which shall have passed the House of Representatives and the Senate, shall, before it become a Law, be presented to the President of the United States; If he approve he shall sign it, but if not he shall return it, with his Objections to that House in which it shall have originated, who shall enter the Objections at large on their Journal, and proceed to reconsider it. If after such Reconsideration two thirds of that House shall agree to pass the Bill, it shall be sent, together with the Objections, to the other House, by which it shall likewise be reconsidered, and if approved by two thirds of that House, it shall become a Law. But in all such Cases the Votes of both Houses shall be determined by Yeas and Nays, and the Names of the Persons voting for and against the Bill shall be entered on the Journal of each House respectively. If any Bill shall not be returned by the President within ten Days (Sundays excepted) after it shall have been presented to him, the Same shall be a Law, in like Manner as if he had signed it, unless the Congress by their Adjournment prevent its Return, in which Case it shall not be a Law.

Every Order, Resolution, or Vote to which the Concurrence of the Senate and House of Representatives may be necessary (except on a question of Adjournment) shall be presented to the President of the United States; and before the Same shall take Effect, shall be approved by him, or being disapproved by him, shall be repassed by two thirds of the Senate and House of Representatives, according to the Rules and Limitations prescribed in the Case of a Bill.

Section 8. Powers of Congress

The Congress shall have Power To lay and collect Taxes, Duties, Imposts and Excises, to pay the Debts and provide for the common Defence and general Welfare of the United States; but all Duties, Imposts and Excises shall be uniform throughout the United States;

To borrow Money on the credit of the United States;

To regulate Commerce with foreign Nations, and among the several States, and with the Indian Tribes;

To establish an uniform Rule of Naturalization, and uniform Laws on the subject of Bankruptcies throughout the United States;

To coin Money, regulate the Value thereof, and of foreign Coin, and fix the Standard of Weights and Measures;

To provide for the Punishment of counterfeiting the Securities and current Coin of the United States;

To establish Post Offices and post Roads;

To promote the Progress of Science and useful Arts, by securing for limited Times to Authors and Inventors the exclusive Right to their respective Writings and Discoveries;

To constitute Tribunals inferior to the supreme Court;

To define and punish Piracies and Felonies committed on the high Seas, and Offences against the Law of Nations;

To declare War, grant Letters of Marque and Reprisal, and make Rules concerning Captures on Land and Water;

To raise and support Armies, but no Appropriation of Money to that Use shall be for a longer Term than two Years;

To provide and maintain a Navy;

To make Rules for the Government and Regulation of the land and naval Forces;

To provide for calling forth the Militia to execute the Laws of the Union, suppress Insurrections and repel Invasions;

To provide for organizing, arming, and disciplining the Militia, and for governing such Part of them as may be employed in the Service of the United States, reserving to the States respectively, the Appointment of the Officers, and the Authority of training the Militia according to the discipline prescribed by Congress;

To exercise exclusive Legislation in all Cases whatsoever, over such District (not exceeding ten Miles square) as may, by Cession of particular States, and the acceptance of Congress, become the Seat of the Government of the United States, and to exercise like Authority over all Places purchased by the Consent of the Legislature of the State in which the Same shall be, for the Erection of Forts, Magazines, Arsenals, dock-Yards, and other needful Buildings—And

To make all Laws which shall be necessary and proper for carrying into Execution the foregoing Powers, and all other Powers vested by this Constitution in the Government of the United States, or in any Department or Officer thereof.

Section 9. Limits on Congress

The Migration or Importation of such Persons as any of the States now existing shall think proper to admit, shall not be prohibited by the Congress prior to the Year one thousand eight hundred and eight, but a Tax or duty may be imposed on such Importation, not exceeding ten dollars for each Person.

The privilege of the Writ of Habeas Corpus shall not be suspended, unless when in Cases of Rebellion or Invasion the public Safety may require it.

No Bill of Attainder or ex post facto Law shall be passed.

No Capitation, or other direct, Tax shall be laid, unless in Proportion to the Census or enumeration herein before directed to be taken.

No Tax or Duty shall be laid on Articles exported from any State.

No Preference shall be given by any Regulation of Commerce or Revenue to the Ports of one State over those of another: nor shall Vessels bound to, or from, one State, be obliged to enter, clear, or pay Duties in another.

No Money shall be drawn from the Treasury, but in Consequence of Appropriations made by Law; and a regular Statement and Account of the Receipts and Expenditures of all public Money shall be published from time to time.

No Title of Nobility shall be granted by the United States: And no Person holding any Office of Profit or Trust under them, shall, without the Consent of the Congress, accept of any present, Emolument, Office, or Title, of any kind whatever, from any King, Prince, or foreign State.

Section 10. Powers Prohibited of States

No State shall enter into any Treaty, Alliance, or Confederation; grant Letters of Marque and Reprisal; coin Money; emit Bills of Credit; make any Thing but gold and silver Coin a Tender in Payment of Debts; pass any Bill of Attainder, ex post facto Law, or Law impairing the Obligation of Contracts, or grant any Title of Nobility.

No State shall, without the Consent of the Congress, lay any Imposts or Duties on Imports or Exports, except what may be absolutely necessary for executing it's inspection Laws: and the net Produce of all Duties and Imposts, laid by any State on Imports or Exports, shall be for the Use of the Treasury of the United States; and all such Laws shall be subject to the Revision and Controul of the Congress.

No State shall, without the Consent of Congress, lay any Duty of Tonnage, keep Troops, or Ships of War in time of Peace, enter into any Agreement or Compact with another State, or with a foreign Power, or engage in War, unless actually invaded, or in such imminent Danger as will not admit of delay.

Article II. The Executive Branch

Section 1. The President

The executive Power shall be vested in a President of the United States of America. He shall hold his Office during the Term of four Years, and, together with the Vice President, chosen for the same Term, be elected, as follows:

Each State shall appoint, in such Manner as the Legislature thereof may direct, a Number of Electors, equal to the whole Number of Senators and Representatives to which the State may be entitled in the Congress: but no Senator or Representative, or Person holding an Office of Trust or Profit under the United States, shall be appointed an Elector.

The Electors shall meet in their respective States, and vote by Ballot for two persons, of whom one at least shall not lie an Inhabitant of the same State with themselves. And they shall make a List of all the Persons voted for, and of the Number of Votes for each; which List they shall sign and certify, and transmit sealed to the Seat of the Government of the United States, directed to the President of the Senate. The President of the Senate shall, in the Presence of the Senate and House of Representatives, open all the Certificates, and the Votes shall then be counted. The Person having the greatest Number of Votes shall be the President, if such Number be a Majority of the whole Number of Electors appointed; and if there be more than one who have such Majority, and have an equal Number of Votes, then the House of Representatives shall immediately choose by Ballot one of them for President; and if no Person have a Majority, then from the five highest on the List the said House shall in like Manner chuse the President. But in chusing the President, the Votes shall be taken by States, the Representation from each State having one Vote; a quorum for this purpose shall consist of a Member or Members from two thirds of the States, and a Majority of all the States shall be necessary to a Choice. In every Case, after the Choice of the President, the Person having the greatest Number of Votes of the Electors shall be the Vice President. But if there should remain two or more who have equal Votes, the Senate shall chuse from them by Ballot the Vice President.

The Congress may determine the Time of chusing the Electors, and the Day on which they shall give their Votes; which Day shall be the same throughout the United States.

No person except a natural born Citizen, or a Citizen of the United States, at the time of the Adoption of this Constitution, shall be eligible to the Office of President; neither shall any Person be eligible to that Office who shall not have attained to the Age of thirty five Years, and been fourteen Years a Resident within the United States.

In Case of the Removal of the President from Office, or of his Death, Resignation, or Inability to discharge the Powers and Duties of the said Office, the Same shall devolve on the Vice President, and the Congress may by Law provide for the Case of Removal, Death, Resignation or Inability, both of the President and Vice President, declaring what Officer shall then act as President, and such Officer shall act accordingly, until the Disability be removed, or a President shall be elected.

The President shall, at stated Times, receive for his Services, a Compensation, which shall neither be increased nor diminished during the Period for which he shall have been elected, and he shall not receive within that Period any other Emolument from the United States, or any of them.

Before he enter on the Execution of his Office, he shall take the following Oath or Affirmation—"I do solemnly swear (or affirm) that I will faithfully execute the Office of President of the United States, and will to the best of my Ability, preserve, protect and defend the Constitution of the United States."

Section 2. Civilian Power over Military, Cabinet, Pardon Power, Appointments

The President shall be Commander in Chief of the Army and Navy of the United States, and of the Militia of the several States, when called into the actual Service of the United States; he may require the Opinion, in writing, of the principal Officer in each of the executive Departments, upon any Subject relating to the Duties of their respective Offices, and he shall have Power to grant Reprieves and Pardons for Offences against the United States, except in Cases of Impeachment.

He shall have Power, by and with the Advice and Consent of the Senate, to make Treaties, provided two thirds of the Senators present concur; and he shall nominate, and by and with the Advice and Consent of the Senate, shall appoint Ambassadors, other public Ministers and Consuls, Judges of the supreme Court, and all other Officers of the United States, whose Appointments are not herein otherwise provided for, and which shall be established by Law: but the Congress may by Law vest the Appointment of such inferior Officers, as they think proper, in the President alone, in the Courts of Law, or in the Heads of Departments.

The President shall have Power to fill up all Vacancies that may happen during the Recess of the Senate, by granting Commissions which shall expire at the End of their next Session.

Section 3. State of the Union, Convening Congress

He shall from time to time give to the Congress Information of the State of the Union, and recommend to their Consideration such Measures as he shall judge necessary and expedient; he may, on extraordinary Occasions, convene both Houses, or either of them, and in Case of Disagreement between them, with Respect to the Time of Adjournment, he may adjourn them to such Time as he shall think proper; he shall receive Ambassadors and other public Ministers; he shall take Care that the Laws be faithfully executed, and shall Commission all the Officers of the United States.

Section 4. Disqualification

The President, Vice President and all civil Officers of the United States, shall be removed from Office on Impeachment for, and Conviction of, Treason, Bribery, or other high Crimes and Misdemeanors.

Article III. The Judicial Branch

Section 1. Judicial Powers

The judicial Power of the United States, shall be vested in one supreme Court, and in such inferior Courts as the Congress may from time to time ordain and establish. The Judges, both of the supreme and inferior Courts, shall hold their Offices during good Behaviour, and shall, at stated Times, receive for their Services a Compensation, which shall not be diminished during their Continuance in Office.

Section 2. Trial by Jury, Original Jurisdiction, Jury Trials

The judicial Power shall extend to all Cases, in Law and Equity, arising under this Constitution, the Laws of the United States, and Treaties made, or which shall be made, under their Authority—to all Cases affecting Ambassadors, other public Ministers and Consuls—to all Cases of admiralty and maritime Jurisdiction—to Controversies to which the United States shall be a Party; to Controversies between two or more States—between a State and Citizens of another State—between Citizens of different States—between Citizens of the same State claiming Lands under Grants of different States, and between a State, or the Citizens thereof, and foreign States, Citizens or Subjects.

In all Cases affecting Ambassadors, other public Ministers and Consuls, and those in which a State shall be Party, the supreme Court shall have original Jurisdiction. In all the other Cases before mentioned, the supreme Court shall have appellate Jurisdiction, both as to Law and Fact, with such Exceptions, and under such Regulations as the Congress shall make.

The Trial of all Crimes, except in Cases of Impeachment, shall be by Jury; and such Trial shall be held in the State where the said Crimes shall have been committed; but when not committed within any State, the Trial shall be at such Place or Places as the Congress may by Law have directed.

Section 3. Treason

Treason against the United States, shall consist only in levying War against them, or in adhering to their Enemies, giving them Aid and Comfort. No Person shall be convicted of Treason unless on the Testimony of two Witnesses to the same overt Act, or on Confession in open Court.

The Congress shall have power to declare the Punishment of Treason, but no Attainder of Treason shall work Corruption of Blood, or Forfeiture except during the Life of the Person attainted.

Article IV. The States

Section 1. Each State to Honor All Others

Full Faith and Credit shall be given in each State to the public Acts, Records, and judicial Proceedings of every other State. And the Congress may by general Laws prescribe the Manner in which such Acts, Records and Proceedings shall be proved, and the Effect thereof.

Section 2. State Citizens, Extradition

The Citizens of each State shall be entitled to all Privileges and Immunities of Citizens in the several States.

A Person charged in any State with Treason, Felony, or other Crime, who shall flee from Justice, and be found in another State, shall on Demand of the executive Authority of the State from which he fled, be delivered up, to be removed to the State having Jurisdiction of the Crime.

No Person held to Service or Labour in one State, under the Laws thereof, escaping into another, shall, in Consequence of any Law or Regulation therein, be discharged from such Service or Labour, but shall be delivered up on Claim of the Party to whom such Service or Labour may be due.

Section 3. New States

New States may be admitted by the Congress into this Union; but no new State shall be formed or erected within the Jurisdiction of any other State; nor any State be formed by the Junction of two or more States, or parts of States, without the Consent of the Legislatures of the States concerned as well as of the Congress.

The Congress shall have Power to dispose of and make all needful Rules and Regulations respecting the Territory or other Property belonging to the United States; and nothing in this Constitution shall be so construed as to Prejudice any Claims of the United States, or of any particular State.

Section 4. Republican Government

The United States shall guarantee to every State in this Union a Republican Form of Government, and shall protect each of them against Invasion; and on Application of the Legislature, or of the Executive (when the Legislature cannot be convened) against domestic Violence.

Article V. Amendment

The Congress, whenever two thirds of both Houses shall deem it necessary, shall propose Amendments to this Constitution, or, on the Application of the Legislatures of two thirds of the several States, shall call a Convention for proposing Amendments, which, in either Case, shall be valid to all Intents and Purposes, as Part of this Constitution, when ratified by the Legislatures of three fourths of the several States, or by Conventions in three fourths thereof, as the one or the other Mode of Ratification may be proposed by the Congress; Provided that no Amendment which may be made prior to the Year One thousand eight hundred and eight shall in any Manner affect the first and fourth Clauses in the Ninth Section of the first Article; and that no State, without its Consent, shall be deprived of its equal Suffrage in the Senate.

Article VI. Debts, Supremacy, Oaths

All Debts contracted and Engagements entered into, before the Adoption of this Constitution, shall be as valid against the United States under this Constitution, as under the Confederation.

This Constitution, and the Laws of the United States which shall be made in Pursuance thereof; and all Treaties made, or which shall be made, under the Authority of the United States, shall be the supreme Law of the Land; and the Judges in every State shall be bound thereby, any Thing in the Constitution or Laws of any State to the Contrary notwithstanding.

The Senators and Representatives before mentioned, and the Members of the several State Legislatures, and all executive and judicial Officers, both of the United States and of the several States, shall be bound by Oath or Affirmation, to support this Constitution; but no religious Test shall ever be required as a Qualification to any Office or public Trust under the United States.

Article VII. Ratification

The Ratification of the Conventions of nine States, shall be sufficient for the Establishment of this Constitution between the States so ratifying the Same.

The Word, "the," being interlined between the seventh and eighth Lines of the first Page, the Word "Thirty" being partly written on an Erazure in the fifteenth Line of the first Page, The Words "is tried" being interlined between the thirty second and thirty third Lines of the first Page and the Word "the" being interlined between the forty third and forty fourth Lines of the second Page.

Attest William Jackson Secretary

Done in Convention by the Unanimous Consent of the States present the Seventeenth Day of September in the Year of our Lord one thousand seven hundred and Eighty seven and of the Independence of the United States of America the Twelfth In witness whereof We have hereunto subscribed our Names,

G°. Washington
Presidt and deputy from Virginia

Delaware
Geo: Read
Gunning Bedford jun
John Dickinson
Richard Bassett
Jaco: Broom

Maryland
James McHenry

Dan of St Thos. Jenifer
Danl. Carroll

Virginia
John Blair
James Madison Jr.

North Carolina
Wm. Blount
Richd. Dobbs Spaight
Hu Williamson

South Carolina
J. Rutledge
Charles Cotesworth Pinckney
Charles Pinckney
Pierce Butler

Georgia
William Few
Abr Baldwin

New Hampshire
John Langdon
Nicholas Gilman

Massachusetts
Nathaniel Gorham
Rufus King

Connecticut
Wm. Saml. Johnson
Roger Sherman

New York
Alexander Hamilton

New Jersey
Wil: Livingston
David Brearley
Wm. Paterson
Jona: Dayton

Pennsylvania
B Franklin
Thomas Mifflin
Robt. Morris
Geo. Clymer
Thos. FitzSimons
Jared Ingersoll
James Wilson
Gouv Morris

* * *

The Amendments

The following are the Amendments to the Constitution. The first ten Amendments collectively are commonly known as the **Bill of Rights.**

Amendment I. Freedom of Religion, Press, Expression

Congress shall make no law respecting an establishment of religion, or prohibiting the free exercise thereof; or abridging the freedom of speech, or of the press; or the right of the people peaceably to assemble, and to petition the Government for a redress of grievances.

Amendment II. Right to Bear Arms

A well regulated Militia, being necessary to the security of a free State, the right of the people to keep and bear Arms, shall not be infringed.

Amendment III. Quartering of Soldiers

No Soldier shall, in time of peace be quartered in any house, without the consent of the Owner, nor in time of war, but in a manner to be prescribed by law.

Amendment IV. Search and Seizure

The right of the people to be secure in their persons, houses, papers, and effects, against unreasonable searches and seizures, shall not be violated, and no Warrants shall issue, but upon probable cause, supported by Oath or affirmation, and particularly describing the place to be searched, and the persons or things to be seized.

Amendment V. Trial and Punishment, Compensation for Takings

No person shall be held to answer for a capital, or otherwise infamous crime, unless on a presentment or indictment of a Grand Jury, except in cases arising in the land or naval forces, or in the Militia, when in actual service in time of War or public danger; nor shall any person be subject for the same offense to be twice put in jeopardy of life or limb; nor shall be compelled in any criminal case to be a witness against himself, nor be deprived of life, liberty, or property, without due process of law; nor shall private property be taken for public use, without just compensation.

Amendment VI. Right to Speedy Trial, Confrontation of Witnesses

In all criminal prosecutions, the accused shall enjoy the right to a speedy and public trial, by an impartial jury of the State and district wherein the crime shall have been committed, which district shall have been previously ascertained by law, and to be informed of the nature and cause of the accusation; to be confronted with the witnesses against him; to have compulsory process for obtaining witnesses in his favor, and to have the Assistance of Counsel for his defence.

Amendment VII. Trial by Jury in Civil Cases

In Suits at common law, where the value in controversy shall exceed twenty dollars, the right of trial by jury shall be preserved, and no fact tried by a jury, shall be otherwise re-examined in any Court of the United States, than according to the rules of the common law.

Amendment VIII. Cruel and Unusual Punishment

Excessive bail shall not be required, nor excessive fines imposed, nor cruel and unusual punishments inflicted.

Amendment IX. Construction of Constitution

The enumeration in the Constitution, of certain rights, shall not be construed to deny or disparage others retained by the people.

Amendment X. Powers of the States and People.

The powers not delegated to the United States by the Constitution, nor prohibited by it to the States, are reserved to the States respectively, or to the people.

Amendment XI. Judicial Limits

The Judicial power of the United States shall not be construed to extend to any suit in law or equity, commenced or prosecuted against one of the United States by Citizens of another State, or by Citizens or Subjects of any Foreign State.

Amendment XII. Choosing the President, Vice-President

The Electors shall meet in their respective states, and vote by ballot for President and Vice-President, one of whom, at least, shall not be an inhabitant of the same state with themselves; they shall name in their ballots the person voted for as President, and in distinct ballots the person voted for as Vice-President, and they shall make distinct lists of all persons voted for as President, and of all persons voted for as Vice-President and of the number of votes for each, which lists they shall sign and certify, and transmit sealed to the seat of the government of the United States, directed to the President of the Senate;

The President of the Senate shall, in the presence of the Senate and House of Representatives, open all the certificates and the votes shall then be counted;

The person having the greatest Number of votes for President, shall be the President, if such number be a majority of the whole number of Electors appointed; and if no person have such majority, then from the persons having the highest numbers not exceeding three on the list of those voted for as President, the House of Representatives shall choose immediately, by ballot, the President. But in choosing the President, the votes shall be taken by states, the representation from each state having one vote; a quorum for this purpose shall consist of a member or members from two-thirds of the states, and a majority of all the states shall be necessary to a choice. And if the House of Representatives shall not choose a President whenever the right of choice shall devolve upon them, before the fourth day of March next following, then the Vice-President shall act as President, as in the case of the death or other constitutional disability of the President.

The person having the greatest number of votes as Vice-President, shall be the Vice-President, if such number be a majority of the whole number of Electors appointed, and if no person have a majority, then from the two highest numbers on the list, the Senate shall choose the Vice-President; a quorum for the purpose shall consist of two-thirds of the whole number of Senators, and a majority of the whole number shall be necessary to a choice. But no person constitutionally ineligible to the office of President shall be eligible to that of Vice-President of the United States.

Amendment XIII. Slavery Abolished.

1. Neither slavery nor involuntary servitude, except as a punishment for crime whereof the party shall have been duly convicted, shall exist within the United States, or any place subject to their jurisdiction.

2. Congress shall have power to enforce this article by appropriate legislation.

Amendment XIV. Citizenship Rights.

1. All persons born or naturalized in the United States, and subject to the jurisdiction thereof, are citizens of the United States and of the State wherein they reside. No State shall make or enforce any law which shall abridge the privileges or immunities of citizens of the United States; nor shall any State deprive any person of life, liberty, or property, without due process of law; nor deny to any person within its jurisdiction the equal protection of the laws.

2. Representatives shall be apportioned among the several States according

to their respective numbers, counting the whole number of persons in each State, excluding Indians not taxed. But when the right to vote at any election for the choice of electors for President and Vice-President of the United States, Representatives in Congress, the Executive and Judicial officers of a State, or the members of the Legislature thereof, is denied to any of the male inhabitants of such State, being twenty-one years of age, and citizens of the United States, or in any way abridged, except for participation in rebellion, or other crime, the basis of representation therein shall be reduced in the proportion which the number of such male citizens shall bear to the whole number of male citizens twenty-one years of age in such State.

3. No person shall be a Senator or Representative in Congress, or elector of President and Vice-President, or hold any office, civil or military, under the United States, or under any State, who, having previously taken an oath, as a member of Congress, or as an officer of the United States, or as a member of any State legislature, or as an executive or judicial officer of any State, to support the Constitution of the United States, shall have engaged in insurrection or rebellion against the same, or given aid or comfort to the enemies thereof. But Congress may by a vote of two-thirds of each House, remove such disability.

4. The validity of the public debt of the United States, authorized by law, including debts incurred for payment of pensions and bounties for services in suppressing insurrection or rebellion, shall not be questioned. But neither the United States nor any State shall assume or pay any debt or obligation incurred in aid of insurrection or rebellion against the United States, or any claim for the loss or emancipation of any slave; but all such debts, obligations and claims shall be held illegal and void.

5. The Congress shall have power to enforce, by appropriate legislation, the provisions of this article.

Amendment XV. Race No Bar to Vote.

1. The right of citizens of the United States to vote shall not be denied or

abridged by the United States or by any State on account of race, color, or previous condition of servitude—

2. The Congress shall have power to enforce this article by appropriate legislation.

Amendment XVI. Status of Income Tax Clarified.

The Congress shall have power to lay and collect taxes on incomes, from whatever source derived, without apportionment among the several States, and without regard to any census or enumeration.

Amendment XVII. Senators Elected by Popular Vote.

The Senate of the United States shall be composed of two Senators from each State, elected by the people thereof, for six years; and each Senator shall have one vote. The electors in each State shall have the qualifications requisite for electors of the most numerous branch of the State legislatures.

When vacancies happen in the representation of any State in the Senate, the executive authority of such State shall issue writs of election to fill such vacancies: *Provided,* That the legislature of any State may empower the executive thereof to make temporary appointments until the people fill the vacancies by election as the legislature may direct.

This amendment shall not be so construed as to affect the election or term of any Senator chosen before it becomes valid as part of the Constitution.

Amendment XVIII. Liquor Abolished.

1. After one year from the ratification of this article the manufacture, sale, or transportation of intoxicating liquors within, the importation thereof into, or the exportation thereof from the United States and all territory subject to the jurisdiction thereof for beverage purposes is hereby prohibited.

2. The Congress and the several States shall have concurrent power to enforce this article by appropriate legislation.

3. This article shall be inoperative unless it shall have been ratified as an amendment to the Constitution by the legislatures of the several States, as provided in the Constitution, within seven years from the date of the submission hereof to the States by the Congress.

Amendment XIX. Women's Suffrage.

The right of citizens of the United States to vote shall not be denied or abridged by the United States or by any State on account of sex.

Congress shall have power to enforce this article by appropriate legislation.

Amendment XX. Presidential, Congressional Terms.

1. The terms of the President and Vice President shall end at noon on the 20th day of January, and the terms of Senators and Representatives at noon on the 3d day of January, of the years in which such terms would have ended if this article had not been ratified; and the terms of their successors shall then begin.

2. The Congress shall assemble at least once in every year, and such meeting shall begin at noon on the 3d day of January, unless they shall by law appoint a different day.

3. If, at the time fixed for the beginning of the term of the President, the President elect shall have died, the Vice President elect shall become President. If a President shall not have been chosen before the time fixed for the beginning of his term, or if the President elect shall have failed to qualify, then the Vice President elect shall act as President until a President shall have qualified; and the Congress may by law provide for the case wherein neither a President elect nor a Vice President elect shall have qualified, declaring who shall then act as President, or the manner in which one who is to act shall be selected, and such person shall act accordingly until a President or Vice President shall have qualified.

4. The Congress may by law provide for the case of the death of any of the persons from whom the House of Representatives may choose a President whenever the right of choice shall have devolved upon them,

and for the case of the death of any of the persons from whom the Senate may choose a Vice President whenever the right of choice shall have devolved upon them.

5. Sections 1 and 2 shall take effect on the 15th day of October following the ratification of this article.

6. This article shall be inoperative unless it shall have been ratified as an amendment to the Constitution by the legislatures of three-fourths of the several States within seven years from the date of its submission.

Amendment XXI. Amendment XVIII Repealed.

1. The eighteenth article of amendment to the Constitution of the United States is hereby repealed.

2. The transportation or importation into any State, Territory, or possession of the United States for delivery or use therein of intoxicating liquors, in violation of the laws thereof, is hereby prohibited.

3. The article shall be inoperative unless it shall have been ratified as an amendment to the Constitution by conventions in the several States, as provided in the Constitution, within seven years from the date of the submission hereof to the States by the Congress.

Amendment XXII. Presidential Term Limits.

1. No person shall be elected to the office of the President more than twice, and no person who has held the office of President, or acted as President, for more than two years of a term to which some other person was elected President shall be elected to the office of the President more than once. But this Article shall not apply to any person holding the office of President, when this Article was proposed by the Congress, and shall not prevent any person who may be holding the office of President, or acting as President, during the term within which this Article becomes operative from holding the office of President or acting as President during the remainder of such term.

2. This article shall be inoperative unless it shall have been ratified as an amendment to the Constitution by the legislatures of three-fourths of the several States within seven years from the date of its submission to the States by the Congress.

Amendment XXIII. Presidential Vote for District of Columbia.

1. The District constituting the seat of Government of the United States shall appoint in such manner as the Congress may direct:

   A number of electors of President and Vice President equal to the whole number of Senators and Representatives in Congress to which the District would be entitled if it were a State, but in no event more than the least populous State; they shall be in addition to those appointed by the States, but they shall be considered, for the purposes of the election of President and Vice President, to be electors appointed by a State; and they shall meet in the District and perform such duties as provided by the twelfth article of amendment.

2. The Congress shall have power to enforce this article by appropriate legislation.

Amendment XXIV. Poll Tax Barred.

1. The right of citizens of the United States to vote in any primary or other election for President or Vice President, for electors for President or Vice President, or for Senator or Representative in Congress, shall not be denied or abridged by the United States or any State by reason of failure to pay any poll tax or other tax.

2. The Congress shall have power to enforce this article by appropriate legislation.

Amendment XXV. Presidential Disability and Succession.

1. In case of the removal of the President from office or of his death or resignation, the Vice President shall become President.

2. Whenever there is a vacancy in the office of the Vice President, the

President shall nominate a Vice President who shall take office upon confirmation by a majority vote of both Houses of Congress.

3. Whenever the President transmits to the President pro tempore of the Senate and the Speaker of the House of Representatives his written declaration that he is unable to discharge the powers and duties of his office, and until he transmits to them a written declaration to the contrary, such powers and duties shall be discharged by the Vice President as Acting President.

4. Whenever the Vice President and a majority of either the principal officers of the executive departments or of such other body as Congress may by law provide, transmit to the President pro tempore of the Senate and the Speaker of the House of Representatives their written declaration that the President is unable to discharge the powers and duties of his office, the Vice President shall immediately assume the powers and duties of the office as Acting President.

Thereafter, when the President transmits to the President pro tempore of the Senate and the Speaker of the House of Representatives his written declaration that no inability exists, he shall resume the powers and duties of his office unless the Vice President and a majority of either the principal officers of the executive department or of such other body as Congress may by law provide, transmit within four days to the President pro tempore of the Senate and the Speaker of the House of Representatives their written declaration that the President is unable to discharge the powers and duties of his office. Thereupon Congress shall decide the issue, assembling within forty-eight hours for that purpose if not in session. If the Congress, within twenty-one days after receipt of the latter written declaration, or, if Congress is not in session, within twenty-one days after Congress is required to assemble, determines by two-thirds vote of both Houses that the President is unable to discharge the powers and duties of his office, the Vice President shall continue to discharge the same as Acting President; otherwise, the President shall resume the powers and duties of his office.

Amendment XXVI. Voting Age Set to 18 Years.

1. The right of citizens of the United States, who are eighteen years of age or older, to vote shall not be denied or abridged by the United States or by any State on account of age.

2. The Congress shall have power to enforce this article by appropriate legislation.

Amendment XXVII. Limiting Congressional Pay Increases.

No law, varying the compensation for the services of the Senators and Representatives, shall take effect, until an election of Representatives shall have intervened.

* * *

Appendix B

The Charter of the United Nations

Preamble

We the Peoples of the United Nations Determined

to save succeeding generations from the scourge of war, which twice in our lifetime has brought untold sorrow to mankind, and
to reaffirm faith in fundamental human rights, in the dignity and worth of the human person, in the equal rights of men and women and of nations large and small, and
to establish conditions under which justice and respect for the obligations arising from treaties and other sources of international law can be maintained, and
to promote social progress and better standards of life in larger freedom,

And for these Ends

to practice tolerance and live together in peace with one another as good neighbors, and
to unite our strength to maintain international peace and security, and
to ensure by the acceptance of principles and the institution of methods, that armed force shall not be used, save in the common interest,
and to employ international machinery for the promotion of the economic and social advancement of all peoples,

Have Resolved to Combine our Efforts to Accomplish these Aims

Accordingly, our respective Governments, through representatives assembled in the city of San Francisco, who have exhibited their full powers found to be in good and due form, have agreed to the present Charter of the United Nations and do hereby establish an international organization to be known as the United Nations.

Chapter I. Purposes and Principles

Article 1

The Purposes of the United Nations are:

1. To maintain international peace and security, and to that end: to take effective collective measures for the prevention and removal of threats to the peace, and for the suppression of acts of aggression or other breaches of the peace, and to bring about by peaceful means, and in conformity with the principles of justice and international law, adjustment or settlement of international disputes or situations which might lead to a breach of the peace;

2. To develop friendly relations among nations based on respect for the principle of equal rights and self-determination of peoples, and to take other appropriate measures to strengthen universal peace;

3. To achieve international co-operation in solving international problems of an economic, social, cultural, or humanitarian character, and in promoting and encouraging respect for human rights and for fundamental freedoms for all without distinction as to race, sex, language, or religion; and

4. To be a centre for harmonizing the actions of nations in the attainment of these common ends.

Article 2

The Organization and its Members, in pursuit of the Purposes stated in Article 1, shall act in accordance with the following Principles.

1. The Organization is based on the principle of the sovereign equality of all its Members.

2. All Members, in order to ensure to all of them the rights and benefits resulting from membership, shall fulfill in good faith the obligations assumed by them in accordance with the present Charter.

3. All Members shall settle their international disputes by peaceful means in such a manner that international peace and security, and justice, are not endangered.

4. All Members shall refrain in their international relations from the threat or use of force against the territorial integrity or political independence of any state, or in any other manner inconsistent with the Purposes of the United Nations.

5. All Members shall give the United Nations every assistance in any action it takes in accordance with the present Charter, and shall refrain from giving assistance to any state against which the United Nations is taking preventive or enforcement action.

6. The Organization shall ensure that states which are not Members of the United Nations act in accordance with these Principles so far as may be necessary for the maintenance of international peace and security.

7. Nothing contained in the present Charter shall authorize the United Nations to intervene in matters which are essentially within the domestic jurisdiction of any state or shall require the Members to submit such matters to settlement under the present Charter; but this principle shall not prejudice the application of enforcement measures under Chapter VII.

Chapter II. Membership

Article 3

The original Members of the United Nations shall be the states which, having participated in the United Nations Conference on International

Organization at San Francisco, or having previously signed the Declaration by United Nations of 1 January 1942, sign the present Charter and ratify it in accordance with Article 110.

Article 4

1. Membership in the United Nations is open to all other peace-loving states which accept the obligations contained in the present Charter and, in the judgment of the Organization, are able and willing to carry out these obligations.

2. The admission of any such state to membership in the United Nations will be effected by a decision of the General Assembly upon the recommendation of the Security Council.

Article 5

A member of the United Nations against which preventive or enforcement action has been taken by the Security Council may be suspended from the exercise of the rights and privileges of membership by the General Assembly upon the recommendation of the Security Council. The exercise of these rights and privileges may be restored by the Security Council.

Article 6

A Member of the United Nations which has persistently violated the Principles contained in the present Charter may be expelled from the Organization by the General Assembly upon the recommendation of the Security Council.

Chapter III. Organs

Article 7

1. There are established as the principal organs of the United Nations:
   a General Assembly
   a Security Council
   an Economic and Social Council
   a Trusteeship Council
   an International Court of Justice
   and a Secretariat.

2. Such subsidiary organs as may be found necessary may be established in accordance with the present Charter.

Article 8

The United Nations shall place no restrictions on the eligibility of men and women to participate in any capacity and under conditions of equality in its principal and subsidiary organs.

Chapter IV. The General Assembly

Composition

Article 9

1. The General Assembly shall consist of all the Members of the United Nations.

2. Each member shall have not more than five representatives in the General Assembly.

Functions and Powers

Article 10

The General Assembly may discuss any questions or any matters within the scope of the present Charter or relating to the powers and functions of any organs provided for in the present Charter, and, except as provided in Article 12, may make recommendations to the Members of the United Nations or to the Security Council or to both on any such questions or matters.

Article 11

1. The General Assembly may consider the general principles of co-operation in the maintenance of international peace and security, including the principles governing disarmament and the regulation of armaments, and may make recommendations with regard to such principles to the Members or to the Security Council or to both.

2. The General Assembly may discuss any questions relating to the maintenance of international peace and security brought before it by

any Member of the United Nations, or by the Security Council, or by a state which is not a Member of the United Nations in accordance with Article 35, paragraph 2, and, except as provided in Article 12, may make recommendations with regard to any such questions to the state or states concerned or to the Security Council or to both. Any such question on which action is necessary shall be referred to the Security Council by the General Assembly either before or after discussion.

3. The General Assembly may call the attention of the Security Council to situations which are likely to endanger international peace and security.

4. The powers of the General Assembly set forth in this Article shall not limit the general scope of Article 10.

Article 12

1. While the Security Council is exercising in respect of any dispute or situation the functions assigned to it in the present Charter, the General Assembly shall not make any recommendation with regard to that dispute or situation unless the Security Council so requests.

2. The Secretary-General, with the consent of the Security Council, shall notify the General Assembly at each session of any matters relative to the maintenance of international peace and security which are being dealt with by the Security Council and shall similarly notify the General Assembly, or the Members of the United Nations if the General Assembly is not in session, immediately the Security Council ceases to deal with such matters.

Article 13

1. The General Assembly shall initiate studies and make recommendations for the purpose of:

   a. promoting international co-operation in the political field and encouraging the progressive development of international law and its codification;

b. promoting international co-operation in the economic, social, cultural, educational, and health fields, and assisting in the realization of human rights and fundamental freedoms for all without distinction as to race, sex, language, or religion.

2. The further responsibilities, functions and powers of the General Assembly with respect to matters mentioned in paragraph 1(b) above are set forth in Chapters IX and X.

Article 14

Subject to the provisions of Article 12, the General Assembly may recommend measures for the peaceful adjustment of any situation, regardless of origin, which it deems likely to impair the general welfare or friendly relations among nations, including situations resulting from a violation of the provisions of the present Charter setting forth the Purposes and Principles of the United Nations.

Article 15

1. The General Assembly shall receive and consider annual and special reports from the Security Council; these reports shall include an account of the measures that the Security Council has decided upon or taken to maintain international peace and security.

2. The General Assembly shall receive and consider reports from the other organs of the United Nations.

Article 16

The General Assembly shall perform such functions with respect to the international trusteeship system as are assigned to it under Chapters XII and XIII, including the approval of the trusteeship agreements for areas not designated as strategic.

Article 17

1. The General Assembly shall consider and approve the budget of the Organization.

2. The expenses of the Organization shall be borne by the Members as apportioned by the General Assembly.

3. The General Assembly shall consider and approve any financial and budgetary arrangements with specialized agencies referred to in Article 57 and shall examine the administrative budgets of such specialized agencies with a view to making recommendations to the agencies concerned.

Voting

Article 18

1. Each member of the General Assembly shall have one vote.

2. Decisions of the General Assembly on important questions shall be made by a two-thirds majority of the members present and voting. These questions shall include: recommendations with respect to the maintenance of international peace and security, the election of the non-permanent members of the Security Council, the election of the members of the Economic and Social Council, the election of members of the Trusteeship Council in accordance with paragraph 1(c) of Article 86, the admission of new Members to the United Nations, the suspension of the rights and privileges of membership, the expulsion of Members, questions relating to the operation of the trusteeship system, and budgetary questions.

3. Decisions on other questions, including the determination of additional categories of questions to be decided by a two-thirds majority, shall be made by a majority of the members present and voting.

Article 19

A Member of the United Nations which is in arrears in the payment of its financial contributions to the Organization shall have no vote in the General Assembly if the amount of its arrears equals or exceeds the amount of the contributions due from it for the preceding two full years. The General Assembly may, nevertheless, permit such a Member to vote if it is satisfied that the failure to pay is due to conditions beyond the control of the Member.

Procedure

Article 20

The General Assembly shall meet in regular annual sessions and in such special sessions as occasion may require. Special sessions shall be convoked by the Secretary-General at the request of the Security Council or of a majority of the Members of the United Nations.

Article 21

The General Assembly shall adopt its own rules of procedure. It shall elect its President for each session.

Article 22

The General Assembly may establish such subsidiary organs as it deems necessary for the performance of its functions.

Chapter V. The Security Council

Composition

Article 23

1. The Security Council shall consist of fifteen Members of the United Nations. The Republic of China, France, the Union of Soviet Socialist Republics, the United Kingdom of Great Britain and Northern Ireland, and the United States of America shall be permanent members of the Security Council. The General Assembly shall elect ten other Members of the United Nations to be non-permanent members of the Security Council, due regard being specially paid, in the first instance to the contribution of Members of the United Nations to the maintenance of international peace and security and to the other purposes of the Organization, and also to equitable geographical distribution.

2. The non-permanent members of the Security Council shall be elected for a term of two years. In the first election of the non-permanent members after the increase of the membership of the Security Council from eleven to fifteen, two of the four additional members shall be

chosen for a term of one year. A retiring member shall not be eligible for immediate re-election.

3. Each member of the Security Council shall have one representative.

Functions and Powers

Article 24

1. In order to ensure prompt and effective action by the United Nations, its Members confer on the Security Council primary responsibility for the maintenance of international peace and security, and agree that in carrying out its duties under this responsibility the Security Council acts on their behalf.

2. In discharging these duties the Security Council shall act in accordance with the Purposes and Principles of the United Nations. The specific powers granted to the Security Council for the discharge of these duties are laid down in Chapters VI, VII, VIII, and XII.

3. The Security Council shall submit annual and, when necessary, special reports to the General Assembly for its consideration.

Article 25

The Members of the United Nations agree to accept and carry out the decisions of the Security Council in accordance with the present Charter.

Article 26

In order to promote the establishment and maintenance of international peace and security with the least diversion for armaments of the world's human and economic resources, the Security Council shall be responsible for formulating, with the assistance of the Military Staff Committee referred to in Article 47, plans to be submitted to the Members of the United Nations for the establishment of a system for the regulation of armaments.

Voting

Article 27

1. Each member of the Security Council shall have one vote.

2. Decisions of the Security Council on procedural matters shall be made by an affirmative vote of nine members.

3. Decisions of the Security Council on all other matters shall be made by an affirmative vote of nine members including the concurring votes of the permanent members; provided that, in decisions under Chapter VI, and under paragraph 3 of Article 52, a party to a dispute shall abstain from voting.

Procedure

Article 28

1. The Security Council shall be so organized as to be able to function continuously. Each member of the Security Council shall for this purpose be represented at all times at the seat of the Organization.

2. The Security Council shall hold periodic meetings at which each of its members may, if it so desires, be represented by a member of the government or by some other specially designated representative.

3. The Security Council may hold meetings at such places other than the seat of the Organization as in its judgment will best facilitate its work.

Article 29

The Security Council may establish such subsidiary organs as it deems necessary for the performance of its functions.

Article 30

The Security Council shall adopt its own rules of procedure, including the method of selecting its President.

Article 31

Any Member of the United Nations which is not a member of the Security Council may participate, without vote, in the discussion of any question brought before the Security Council whenever the latter considers that the interests of that Member are specially affected.

Article 32

Any Member of the United Nations which is not a member of the Security Council or any state which is not a Member of the United Nations, if it is a party to a dispute under consideration by the Security Council, shall be invited to participate, without vote, in the discussion relating to the dispute. The Security Council shall lay down such conditions as it deems just for the participation of a state which is not a Member of the United Nations.

Chapter VI. Pacific Settlement of Disputes

Article 33

1. The parties to any dispute, the continuance of which is likely to endanger the maintenance of international peace and security, shall, first of all, seek a solution by negotiation, enquiry, mediation, conciliation, arbitration, judicial settlement, resort to regional agencies or arrangements, or other peaceful means of their own choice.

2. The Security Council shall, when it deems necessary, call upon the parties to settle their dispute by such means.

Article 34

The Security Council may investigate any dispute, or any situation which might lead to international friction or give rise to a dispute, in order to determine whether the continuance of the dispute or situation is likely to endanger the maintenance of international peace and security.

Article 35

1. Any Member of the United Nations may bring any dispute, or any situation of the nature referred to in Article 34, to the attention of the Security Council or of the General Assembly.

2. A state which is not a Member of the United Nations may bring to the attention of the Security Council or of the General Assembly any dispute to which it is a party if it accepts in advance, for the purposes of the dispute, the obligations of pacific settlement provided in the present Charter.

3. The proceedings of the General Assembly in respect of matters brought to its attention under this Article will be subject to the provisions of Articles 11 and 12.

Article 36

1. The Security Council may, at any stage of a dispute of the nature referred to in Article 33 or of a situation of like nature, recommend appropriate procedures or methods of adjustment.

2. The Security Council should take into consideration any procedures for the settlement of the dispute which have already been adopted by the parties.

3. In making recommendations under this Article the Security Council should also take into consideration that legal disputes should as a general rule be referred by the parties to the International Court of Justice in accordance with the provisions of the Statute of the Court.

Article 37

1. Should the parties to a dispute of the nature referred to in Article 33 fail to settle it by the means indicated in that Article, they shall refer it to the Security Council.

2. If the Security Council deems that the continuance of the dispute is in fact likely to endanger the maintenance of international peace and security, it shall decide whether to take action under Article 36 or to recommend such terms of settlement as it may consider appropriate.

Article 38

Without prejudice to the provisions of Articles 33 to 37, the Security

Council may, if all the parties to any dispute so request, make recommendations to the parties with a view to a pacific settlement of the dispute.

Chapter VII. Action with Respect to Threats to the Peace, Breaches of the Peace, and Acts of Aggression

Article 39

The Security Council shall determine the existence of any threat to the peace, breach of the peace, or act of aggression and shall make recommendations, or decide what measures shall be taken in accordance with Articles 41 and 42, to maintain or restore international peace and security.

Article 40

In order to prevent an aggravation of the situation, the Security Council may, before making the recommendations or deciding upon the measures provided for in Article 39, call upon the parties concerned to comply with such provisional measures as it deems necessary or desirable. Such provisional measures shall be without prejudice to the rights, claims, or position of the parties concerned. The Security Council shall duly take account of failure to comply with such provisional measures.

Article 41

The Security Council may decide what measures not involving the use of armed force are to be employed to give effect to its decisions, and it may call upon the Members of the United Nations to apply such measures. These may include complete or partial interruption of economic relations and of rail, sea, air, postal, telegraphic, radio, and other means of communication, and the severance of diplomatic relations.

Article 42

Should the Security Council consider that measures provided for in Article 41 would be inadequate or have proved to be inadequate, it may take such action by air, sea, or land forces as may be necessary to maintain or restore international peace and security. Such action may include demonstrations, blockade, and other operations by air, sea, or land forces of Members of the United Nations.

Article 43

1. All Members of the United Nations, in order to contribute to the maintenance of international peace and security, undertake to make available to the Security Council, on its call and in accordance with a special agreement or agreements, armed forces, assistance, and facilities, including rights of passage, necessary for the purpose of maintaining international peace and security.

2. Such agreement or agreements shall govern the numbers and types of forces. their degree of readiness and general location, and the nature of the facilities and assistance to be provided.

3. The agreement or agreements shall be negotiated as soon as possible on the initiative of the Security Council. They shall be concluded between the Security Council and Members or between the Security Council and groups of Members and shall be subject to ratification by the signatory states in accordance with their respective constitutional processes.

Article 44

When the Security Council has decided to use force it shall, before calling upon a Member not represented on it to provide armed forces in fulfillment of the obligations assumed under Article 43, invite that Member, if the Member so desires, to participate in the decisions of the Security Council concerning the employment of contingents of that Member's armed forces.

Article 45

In order to enable the United Nations to take urgent military measures Members shall hold immediately available national air-force contingents for combined international enforcement action. The strength and degree of readiness of these contingents and plans for their combined action shall be determined, within the limits laid down in the special agreement or agreements referred to in Article 43, by the Security Council with the assistance of the Military Staff Committee.

Article 46

Plans for the application of armed force shall be made by the Security Council with the assistance of the Military Staff Committee.

Article 47

1. There shall be established a Military Staff Committee to advise and assist the Security Council on all questions relating to the Security Council's military requirements for the maintenance of international peace and security, the employment and command of forces placed at its disposal, the regulation of armaments, and possible disarmament.

2. The Military Staff Committee shall consist of the Chiefs of Staff of the permanent members of the Security Council or their representatives. Any Member of the United Nations not permanently represented on the Committee shall be invited by the Committee to be associated with it when the efficient discharge of the Committee's responsibilities requires the participation of that Member in its work.

3. The Military Staff Committee shall be responsible under the Security Council for the strategic direction of any armed forces placed at the disposal of the Security Council. Questions relating to the command of such forces shall be worked out subsequently.

4. The Military Staff Committee, with the authorization of the Security Council and after consultation with appropriate regional agencies, may establish regional sub-committees.

Article 48

1. The action required to carry out the decisions of the Security Council for the maintenance of international peace and security shall be taken by all the Members of the United Nations or by some of them, as the Security Council may determine.

2. Such decisions shall be carried out by the Members of the United

Nations directly and through their action in the appropriate international agencies of which they are members.

Article 49

The Members of the United Nations shall join in affording mutual assistance in carrying out the measures decided upon by the Security Council.

Article 50

If preventive or enforcement measures against any state are taken by the Security Council, any other state, whether a Member of the United Nations or not, which finds itself confronted with special economic problems arising from the carrying out of those measures shall have the right to consult the Security Council with regard to a solution of those problems.

Article 51

Nothing in the present Charter shall impair the inherent right of individual or collective self-defence if an armed attack occurs against a Member of the United Nations, until the Security Council has taken measures necessary to maintain international peace and security. Measures taken by Members in the exercise of this right of self-defense shall be immediately reported to the Security Council and shall not in any way affect the authority and responsibility of the Security Council under the present Charter to take at any time such action as it deems necessary in order to maintain or restore international peace and security.

Chapter VIII. Regional Arrangements

Article 52

1. Nothing in the present Charter precludes the existence of regional arrangements or agencies for dealing with such matters relating to the maintenance of international peace and security as are appropriate for regional action, provided that such arrangements or agencies and their activities are consistent with the Purposes and Principles of the United Nations.

2. The Members of the United Nations entering into such arrangements

or constituting such agencies shall make every effort to achieve pacific settlement of local disputes through such regional arrangements or by such regional agencies before referring them to the Security Council.

3. The Security Council shall encourage the development of pacific settlement of local disputes through such regional arrangements or by such regional agencies either on the initiative of the states concerned or by reference from the Security Council.

4. This Article in no way impairs the application of Articles 34 and 35.

Article 53

1. The Security Council shall, where appropriate, utilize such regional arrangements or agencies for enforcement action under its authority. But no enforcement action shall be taken under regional arrangements or by regional agencies without the authorization of the Security Council, with the exception of measures against any enemy state, as defined in paragraph 2 of this Article, provided for pursuant to Article 107 or in regional arrangements directed against renewal of aggressive policy on the part of any such state, until such time as the Organization may, on request of the Governments concerned, be charged with the responsibility for preventing further aggression by such a state.

2. The term enemy state as used in paragraph 1 of this Article applies to any state which during the Second World War has been an enemy of any signatory of the present Charter.

Article 54

The Security Council shall at all times be kept fully informed of activities undertaken or in contemplation under regional arrangements or by regional agencies for the maintenance of international peace and security.

Chapter IX. International Economic and Social Co-operation

Article 55

With a view to the creation of conditions of stability and well-being which are necessary for peaceful and friendly relations among nations based on respect for the principle of equal rights and self-determination of peoples, the United Nations shall promote:

a. higher standards of living, full employment, and conditions of economic and social progress and development;

b. solutions of international economic, social, health, and related problems; and international cultural and educational co-operation; and

c. universal respect for, and observance of, human rights and fundamental freedoms for all without distinction as to race, sex, language, or religion.

Article 56

All Members pledge themselves to take joint and separate action in co-operation with the Organization for the achievement of the purposes set forth in Article 55.

Article 57

1. The various specialized agencies, established by intergovernmental agreement and having wide international responsibilities, as defined in their basic instruments, in economic, social, cultural, educational, health, and related fields, shall be brought into relationship with the United Nations in accordance with the provisions of Article 63.

2. Such agencies thus brought into relationship with the United Nations are hereinafter referred to as specialized agencies.

Article 58

The Organization shall make recommendations for the co-ordination of the policies and activities of the specialized agencies.

Article 59

The Organization shall, where appropriate, initiate negotiations among the states concerned for the creation of any new specialized agencies required for the accomplishment of the purposes set forth in Article 55.

Article 60

Responsibility for the discharge of the functions of the Organization set forth in this Chapter shall be vested in the General Assembly and, under the authority of the General Assembly, in the Economic and Social Council, which shall have for this purpose the powers set forth in Chapter X.

Chapter X. The Economic and Social Council

Composition

Article 61

1. The Economic and Social Council shall consist of fifty-four Members of the United Nations elected by the General Assembly.

2. Subject to the provisions of paragraph 3, eighteen members of the Economic and Social Council shall be elected each year for a term of three years. A retiring member shall be eligible for immediate re-election.

3. At the first election after the increase in the membership of the Economic and Social Council from twenty-seven to fifty-four members, in addition to the members elected in place of the nine members whose term of office expires at the end of that year, twenty-seven additional members shall be elected. Of these twenty-seven additional members, the term of office of nine members so elected shall expire at the end of one year, and of nine other members at the end of two years, in accordance with arrangements made by the General Assembly.

4. Each member of the Economic and Social Council shall have one representative.

Functions and Powers

Article 62

1. The Economic and Social Council may make or initiate studies and reports with respect to international economic, social, cultural, educational, health, and related matters and may make recommendations

with respect to any such matters to the General Assembly, to the Members of the United Nations, and to the specialized agencies concerned.

2. It may make recommendations for the purpose of promoting respect for, and observance of, human rights and fundamental freedoms for all.

3. It may prepare draft conventions for submission to the General Assembly, with respect to matters falling within its competence.

4. It may call, in accordance with the rules prescribed by the United Nations, international conferences on matters falling within its competence.

Article 63

1. The Economic and Social Council may enter into agreements with any of the agencies referred to in Article 57, defining the terms on which the agency concerned shall be brought into relationship with the United Nations. Such agreements shall be subject to approval by the General Assembly.

2. It may co-ordinate the activities of the specialized agencies through consultation with and recommendations to such agencies and through recommendations to the General Assembly and to the Members of the United Nations.

Article 64

1. The Economic and Social Council may take appropriate steps to obtain regular reports from the specialized agencies. It may make arrangements with the Members of the United Nations and with the specialized agencies to obtain reports on the steps taken to give effect to its own recommendations and to recommendations on matters falling within its competence made by the General Assembly.

2. It may communicate its observations on these reports to the General Assembly.

Article 65

The Economic and Social Council may furnish information to the Security Council and shall assist the Security Council upon its request.

Article 66

1. The Economic and Social Council shall perform such functions as fall within its competence in connection with the carrying out of the recommendations of the General Assembly.

2. It may, with the approval of the General Assembly, perform services at the request of Members of the United Nations and at the request of specialized agencies.

3. It shall perform such other functions as are specified elsewhere in the present Charter or as may be assigned to it by the General Assembly.

Voting

Article 67

1. Each member of the Economic and Social Council shall have one vote.

2. Decisions of the Economic and Social Council shall be made by a majority of the members present and voting.

Procedure

Article 68

The Economic and Social Council shall set up commissions in economic and social fields and for the promotion of human rights, and such other commissions as may be required for the performance of its functions.

Article 69

The Economic and Social Council shall invite any Member of the United Nations to participate, without vote, in its deliberations on any matter of particular concern to that Member.

Article 70

The Economic and Social Council may make arrangements for representatives of the specialized agencies to participate, without vote, in its deliberations and in those of the commissions established by it, and for its representatives to participate in the deliberations of the specialized agencies.

Article 71

The Economic and Social Council may make suitable arrangements for consultation with non-governmental organizations which are concerned with matters within its competence. Such arrangements may be made with international organizations and, where appropriate, with national organizations after consultation with the Member of the United Nations concerned.

Article 72

1. The Economic and Social Council shall adopt its own rules of procedure, including the method of selecting its President.

2. The Economic and Social Council shall meet as required in accordance with its rules, which shall include provision for the convening of meetings on the request of a majority of its members.

Chapter XI. Declaration Regarding Non-self-governing Territories

Article 73

Members of the United Nations which have or assume responsibilities for the administration of territories whose peoples have not yet attained a full measure of self-government recognize the principle that the interests of the inhabitants of these territories are paramount, and accept as a sacred trust the obligation to promote to the utmost, within the system of international peace and security established by the present Charter, the well-being of the inhabitants of these territories, and, to this end:

a. to ensure, with due respect for the culture of the peoples concerned, their political, economic, social, and educational advancement, their just treatment, and their protection against abuses;

b. to develop self-government, to take due account of the political aspirations of the peoples, and to assist them in the progressive development of their free political institutions, according to the particular circumstances of each territory and its peoples and their varying stages of advancement;

c. to further international peace and security;

d. to promote constructive measures of development, to encourage research, and to co-operate with one another and, when and where appropriate, with specialized international bodies with a view to the practical achievement of the social, economic, and scientific purposes set forth in this Article; and

e. to transmit regularly to the Secretary-General for information purposes, subject to such limitation as security and constitutional considerations may require, statistical and other information of a technical nature relating to economic, social, and educational conditions in the territories for which they are respectively responsible other than those territories to which Chapter XII and XIII apply.

Article 74

Members of the United Nations also agree that their policy in respect of the territories to which this Chapter applies, no less than in respect of their metropolitan areas, must be based on the general principle of good-neighborliness, due account being taken of the interests and well-being of the rest of the world, in social, economic, and commercial matters.

Chapter XII. International Trusteeship System

Article 75

The United Nations shall establish under its authority an international trusteeship system for the administration and supervision of such territories as may be placed thereunder by subsequent individual agreements. These territories are hereinafter referred to as trust territories.

Article 76

The basic objectives of the trusteeship system, in accordance with the Purposes of the United Nations laid down in Article 1 of the present Charter, shall be:

a. to further international peace and security;

b. to promote the political, economic, social, and educational advancement of the inhabitants of the trust territories, and their progressive development towards self-government or independence as may be appropriate to the particular circumstances of each territory and its peoples and the freely expressed wishes of the peoples concerned, and as may be provided by the terms of each trusteeship agreement;

c. to encourage respect for human rights and for fundamental freedoms for all without distinction as to race, sex, language, or religion, and to encourage recognition of the interdependence of the peoples of the world; and

d. to ensure equal treatment in social, economic, and commercial matters for all Members of the United Nations and their nationals and also equal treatment for the latter in the administration of justice without prejudice to the attainment of the foregoing objectives and subject to the provisions of Article 80.

Article 77

1. The trusteeship system shall apply to such territories in the following categories as may be placed there under by means of trusteeship agreements:

a. territories now held under mandate;

b. territories which may be detached from enemy states as a result of the Second World War, and

c. territories voluntarily placed under the system by states responsible for their administration.

2. It will be a matter for subsequent agreement as to which territories in the foregoing categories will be brought under the trusteeship system and upon what terms.

Article 78

The trusteeship system shall not apply to territories which have become Members of the United Nations, relationship among which shall be based on respect for the principle of sovereign equality.

Article 79

The terms of trusteeship for each territory to be placed under the trusteeship system, including any alteration or amendment, shall be agreed upon by the states directly concerned, including the mandatory power in the case of territories held under mandate by a Member of the United Nations, and shall be approved as provided for in Articles 83 and 85.

Article 80

1. Except as may be agreed upon in individual trusteeship agreements, made under Articles 77, 79, and 81, placing each territory under the trusteeship system, and until such agreements have been concluded, nothing in this Chapter shall be construed in or of itself to alter in any manner the rights whatsoever of any states or any peoples or the terms of existing international instruments to which Members of the United Nations may respectively be parties.

2. Paragraph 1 of this Article shall not be interpreted as giving grounds for delay or postponement of the negotiation and conclusion of agreements for placing mandated and other territories under the trusteeship system as provided for in Article 77.

Article 81

The trusteeship agreement shall in each case include the terms under which the trust territory will be administered and designate the authority which will exercise the administration of the trust territory. Such authority, hereinafter called the administering authority, may be one or more states or the Organization itself.

Article 82

There may be designated, in any trusteeship agreement, a strategic area or areas which may include part or all of the trust territory to which the agreement applies, without prejudice to any special agreement or agreements made under Article 43.

Article 83

1. All functions of the United Nations relating to strategic areas, including the approval of the terms of the trusteeship agreements and of their alteration or amendment, shall be exercised by the Security Council.

2. The basic objectives set forth in Article 76 shall be applicable to the people of each strategic area.

3. The Security Council shall, subject to the provisions of the trusteeship agreements and without prejudice to security considerations, avail itself of the assistance of the Trusteeship Council to perform those functions of the United Nations under the trusteeship system relating to political. economic, social, and educational matters in the strategic areas.

Article 84

It shall be the duty of the administering authority to ensure that the trust territory shall play its part in the maintenance of international peace and security. To this end the administering authority may make use of volunteer forces, facilities, and assistance from the trust territory in carrying out the obligations towards the Security Council undertaken in this regard by the administering authority, as well as for local defense and the maintenance of law and order within the trust territory.

Article 85

1. The functions of the United Nations with regard to trusteeship agreements for all areas not designated as strategic, including the approval of the terms of the trusteeship agreements and of their alteration or amendment, shall be exercised by the General Assembly.

2. The Trusteeship Council, operating under the authority of the General Assembly, shall assist the General Assembly in carrying out these functions.

Chapter XIII. The Trusteeship Council

Composition

Article 86

1. The Trusteeship Council shall consist of the following Members of the United Nations:

a. those Members administering trust territories;

b. such of those Members mentioned by name in Article 23 as are not administering trust territories; and

c. as many other Members elected for three-year terms by the General Assembly as may be necessary to ensure that the total number of members of the Trusteeship Council is equally divided between those Members of the United Nations which administer trust territories and those which do not.

2. Each member of the Trusteeship Council shall designate one specially qualified person to represent it therein.

Functions and Powers

Article 87

The General Assembly and, under its authority, the Trusteeship Council, in carrying out their functions, may:

a. consider reports submitted by the administering authority;

b. accept petitions and examine them in consultation with the administering authority;

c. provide for periodic visits to the respective trust territories at times agreed upon with the administering authority; and

d. take these and other actions in conformity with the terms of the trusteeship agreements.

Article 88

The Trusteeship Council shall formulate a questionnaire on the political, economic, social, and educational advancement of the inhabitants of each trust territory, and the administering authority for each trust territory within the competence of the General Assembly shall make an annual report to the General Assembly upon the basis of such questionnaire.

Voting

Article 89

1. Each member of the Trusteeship Council shall have one vote.

2. Decisions of the Trusteeship Council shall be made by a majority of the members present and voting.

Procedure

Article 90

1. The Trusteeship Council shall adopt its own rules of procedure, including the method of selecting its President.

2. The Trusteeship Council shall meet as required in accordance with its rules, which shall include provision for the convening of meetings on the request of a majority of its members.

Article 91

The Trusteeship Council shall, when appropriate, avail itself of the assistance of the Economic and Social Council and of the specialized agencies in regard to matters with which they are respectively concerned.

Chapter XIV. The International Court of Justice

Article 92

The International Court of Justice shall be the principal judicial organ of the United Nations. It shall function in accordance with the annexed Statute, which is based upon the Statute of the Permanent Court of International Justice and forms an integral part of the present Charter.

Article 93

1. All Members of the United Nations are *ipso facto* parties to the Statute of the International Court of Justice.

2. A state which is not a Member of the United Nations may become a party to the Statute of the International Court of Justice on conditions to be determined in each case by the General Assembly upon the recommendation of the Security Council.

Article 94

1. Each Member of the United Nations undertakes to comply with the decision of the International Court of Justice in any case to which it is a party.

2. If any party to a case fails to perform the obligations incumbent upon it under a judgment rendered by the Court, the other party may have recourse to the Security Council, which may, if it deems necessary, make recommendations or decide upon measures to be taken to give effect to the judgment.

Article 95

Nothing in the present Charter shall prevent Members of the United Nations from entrusting the solution of their differences to other tribunals by virtue of agreements already in existence or which may be concluded in the future.

Article 96

1. The General Assembly or the Security Council may request the International Court of Justice to give an advisory opinion on any legal question.

2. Other organs of the United Nations and specialized agencies, which may at any time be so authorized by the General Assembly, may also request advisory opinions of the Court on legal questions arising within the scope of their activities.

Chapter XV. The Secretariat

Article 97

The Secretariat shall comprise a Secretary-General and such staff as the Organization may require. The Secretary-General shall be appointed by the General Assembly upon the recommendation of the Security Council. He shall be the chief administrative officer of the Organization.

Article 98

The Secretary-General shall act in that capacity in all meetings of the General Assembly, of the Security Council, of the Economic and Social Council, and of the Trusteeship Council, and shall perform such other functions as are entrusted to him by these organs. The Secretary-General shall make an annual report to the General Assembly on the work of the Organization.

Article 99

The Secretary-General may bring to the attention of the Security Council any matter which in his opinion may threaten the maintenance of international peace and security.

Article 100

1. In the performance of their duties the Secretary-General and the staff shall not seek or receive instructions from any government or from any other authority external to the Organization. They shall refrain

from any action which might reflect on their position as international officials responsible only to the Organization.

2. Each Member of the United Nations undertakes to respect the exclusively international character of the responsibilities of the Secretary-General and the staff and not to seek to influence them in the discharge of their responsibilities.

Article 101

1. The staff shall be appointed by the Secretary-General under regulations established by the General Assembly.

2. Appropriate staffs shall be permanently assigned to the Economic and Social Council, the Trusteeship Council, and, as required, to other organs of the United Nations. These staffs shall form a part of the Secretariat.

3. The paramount consideration in the employment of the staff and in the determination of the conditions of service shall be the necessity of securing the highest standards of efficiency, competence, and integrity. Due regard shall be paid to the importance of recruiting the staff on as wide a geographical basis as possible.

Chapter XVI. Miscellaneous Provisions

Article 102

1. Every treaty and every international agreement entered into by any Member of the United Nations after the present Charter comes into force shall as soon as possible be registered with the Secretariat and published by it.

2. No party to any such treaty or international agreement which has not been registered in accordance with the provisions of paragraph 1 of this Article may invoke that treaty or agreement before any organ of the United Nations.

Article 103

In the event of a conflict between the obligations of the Members of the United Nations under the present Charter and their obligations under any other international agreement, their obligations under the present Charter shall prevail.

Article 104

The Organization shall enjoy in the territory of each of its Members such legal capacity as may be necessary for the exercise of its functions and the fulfillment of its purposes.

Article 105

1. The Organization shall enjoy in the territory of each of its Members such privileges and immunities as are necessary for the fulfillment of its purposes.

2. Representatives of the Members of the United Nations and officials of the Organization shall similarly enjoy such privileges and immunities as are necessary for the independent exercise of their functions in connexion with the Organization.

3. The General Assembly may make recommendations with a view to determining the details of the application of paragraphs 1 and 2 of this Article or may propose conventions to the Members of the United Nations for this purpose.

Chapter XVII. Transitional Security Arrangements

Article 106

Pending the coming into force of such special agreements referred to in Article 43 as in the opinion of the Security Council enable it to begin the exercise of its responsibilities under Article 42, the parties to the Four-Nation Declaration, signed at Moscow, 30 October 1943, and France, shall, in accordance with the provisions of paragraph 5 of that Declaration, consult with one another and as occasion requires with other

Members of the United Nations with a view to such joint action on behalf of the Organization as may be necessary for the purpose of maintaining international peace and security.

Article 107

Nothing in the present Charter shall invalidate or preclude action, in relation to any state which during the Second World War has been an enemy of any signatory to the present Charter, taken or authorized as a result of that war by the Governments having responsibility for such action.

Chapter XVIII. Amendments

Article 108

Amendments to the present Charter shall come into force for all Members of the United Nations when they have been adopted by a vote of two thirds of the members of the General Assembly and ratified in accordance with their respective constitutional processes by two thirds of the Members of the United Nations, including all the permanent members of the Security Council.

Article 109

1. A General Conference of the Members of the United Nations for the purpose of reviewing the present Charter may be held at a date and place to be fixed by a two-thirds vote of the members of the General Assembly and by a vote of any seven members of the Security Council. Each Member of the United Nations shall have one vote in the conference.

2. Any alteration of the present Charter recommended by a two-thirds vote of the conference shall take effect when ratified in accordance with their respective constitutional processes by two thirds of the Members of the United Nations including all the permanent members of the Security Council.

3. If such a conference has not been held before the tenth annual session of the General Assembly following the coming into force of the

present Charter, the proposal to call such a conference shall be placed on the agenda of that session of the General Assembly, and the conference shall be held if so decided by a majority vote of the members of the General Assembly and by a vote of any seven members of the Security Council.

Chapter XIX. Ratification and Signature

Article 110

1. The present Charter shall be ratified by the signatory states in accordance with their respective constitutional processes.

2. The ratifications shall be deposited with the Government of the United States of America, which shall notify all the signatory states of each deposit as well as the Secretary-General of the Organization when he has been appointed.

3. The present Charter shall come into force upon the deposit of ratifications by the Republic of China, France, the Union of Soviet Socialist Republics, the United Kingdom of Great Britain and Northern Ireland, and the United States of America, and by a majority of the other signatory states. A protocol of the ratifications deposited shall thereupon be drawn up by the Government of the United States of America which shall communicate copies thereof to all the signatory states.

4. The states signatory to the present Charter which ratify it after it has come into force will become original Members of the United Nations on the date of the deposit of their respective ratifications.

Article 111

The present Charter, of which the Chinese, French, Russian, English, and Spanish texts are equally authentic, shall remain deposited in the archives of the Government of the United States of America. Duly certified copies thereof shall be transmitted by that Government to the Governments of the other signatory states.

IN FAITH WHEREOF the representatives of the Governments of the United Nations have signed the present Charter.

DONE at the city of San Francisco the twenty-sixth day of June, one thousand nine hundred and forty-five.

* * *

Index

action, in OODA-Loop, 47–48, 49. *See also* OODA-Loop
Activist I, II, and III, 81
Ad Hoc Study Group, 36, 37, 38
aerial combat, 41–42
after-action critique, 92
Alinsky, Saul, 94–97
allies vs. supporters, 92
AlterNet.org, 2, 9
anticipation
  of the enemy, 55, 57, 86
  lack of in progressive movement, 89–90
  of your own needs, 86
anticipation of the enemy, 57
Art of War
  after-action critique and, 92
  antiwar movement's need of, 6
  campaigning, art of, 69–71
  global antiwar/peace and justice movement and, 98
  maneuver warfare, 30–35, 36–37, 40
  military service and, 27, 39
  as systematic approach, xiii–xiv
Art of War, The (Sun Tzu), 33, 43, 64
"Art of War for the Antiwar Movement, The" (Ritter), 2–9
Aumand, Maureen, 9–11
battlefield, understanding with IPB, 52–54
battles vs. campaigns, 69–71
benchmarks
  firefighter standard, 22–24, 65, 66, 67
  performance, 69
Blair, Tony, 93
Bonaparte, Napoleon, 12, 13
Boutros-Ghali, Boutros, 15
Boyd, John
  on aerial combat and energy-maneuverability, 41–42
  as father of maneuver warfare, 40
  influences on, 43–45
  OODA-Loop and, 42–43, 46–49, 86
  organic synthesis collective, 43–44, 45–46
Breyman, Steve, 9–11
Bush, George W., 4–5, 90

campaigning, art of, 69–71
Camp Brown, 29
"Camp Casey," 90–91
Camp Upshur, 29
Carlucci, Nick, 35
Caulfield, Matthew, 37
centers of gravity. *See also* core values
  "Camp Casey" and, 91
  Constitution, 98
  core values as, 22

in Gulf War, 37, 38, 39
strategy and, 59
understanding the opponent, 6
chain of command, 77–78
Charter of the United Nations, 98, 127–61
Chase, Colonel, 35
Chen of combat, 43
Chi of combat, 43
"citizen participation," 94, 96, 97
Clausewitz, Carl von
on emotional or psychological factors, 45, 58
on friction, 44–45
on intelligence reports, 35
Marine Corps and, 33
on politics and war, 44
Sun Tzu compared to, 45
command. *See also* leadership
chain of, 77–78
Incident Command System (ICS), 7, 75–79
training in, 75, 77–78, 81
commander's intent, 32–33
CommonDreams.org, 9, 12
communication support teams (CSTs), 84
communication systems and IPB, 53–54
conflict, defined, ii
conflict, life as, xiii–xiv
conflict resolution, xiii–xiv
Constitution of the United States
ignorance of, 25–26
as source of progressive ideals and values, 24–26, 64–65, 97, 98
text of, 105–31
core values. *See also* centers of gravity
constitutional, 24, 64–65, 96–98
of firefighters, 37
need for defining, 21–22
standards and, 81
strategic direction and, 68–69
counter-recruitment movement, 63–68
Crawford, Texas, and "Camp Casey," 90–91
CSTs (communication support teams), 84
cult of personality, 13–14
deceiving the enemy, 33, 64
deciding, in OODA-Loop, 47. *See also* OODA-Loop
decision making
friction and, 46
getting inside decision-cycle of the enemy, 43, 46, 76
IPB process and, 55, 57, 58
OODA-Loop and, 46–49
pro-war movement cycle of, 6–7
Decision-Support Templates (DSTs), 57
Defense Department, 67–68
democracy
citizen participation vs. participatory democracy, 94–97
democratic environment, 16–17
democratization, 15
Democratic Party, 11
demonstrations, 24, 71
Department of Defense, 67–68
doctrinal models, 54–55, 56
DSTs (Decision-Support Templates), 57

elections, November 2006 mid-term, 11, 21
emotional and psychological factors in conflict, 45, 58
enemy or opponent
aggressive tactics toward, 31–32, 60
anticipation of, 55, 57
Clausewitz on, 44
deceiving, 33, 64
event templating and, 55–56
exploiting weaknesses of, 45
friction created for, 49, 70
getting inside decision-cycle of, 43, 46, 76
intelligence on, 34–35
maneuver warfare and, 32–33, 37
pro-war movement as, 6
religious right as, 16
simulations and after-action critique of, 86, 92
understanding through IPB, 54–55
victory over, 87–89

energy-maneuverability, 41
event templating, 55–56

Federal Emergency Management Agency (FEMA), 75–78, 81
ferocity, 88
firefighters
  Incident Command System (ICS) and, 7
  strategy, operations, and tactics, 61–62, 69
  wildland firefighting and ICS, 78–80
firefighter standard or benchmark, 22–24, 65, 66, 67
flat-line organizational model, 73–74, 95
Fleet Marine Force Manual, FMFM-1, *Warfighting* (1989), 36–37, 39–40
"fog of war," 44–45
followership, 78–79, 82
food support teams, 84
Franklin, Benjamin, 73
"Freedom and Justice for All," 24–26
friction
  Clausewitz on, 44–45
  common lexicon and reducing, 77
  counter-recruitment movement and, 67–68
  creating for enemy, 49, 70
  decision-making cycle and, 46
  and life as conflict, xii–xiv
  OODA-Loop and, 48–49
From Followership to Leadership (NWCG course L-280), 79
frontal assaults, 31–32

Gandhi, Mohandas, 13–14
German fighting methods, 31. *See also* Clausewitz, Carl von
global peace and justice movement, 92–94, 97–98
Gray, Al
  Gulf War and maneuver warfare, 36–37, 38–39
  Marine training and maneuver warfare, 30, 32, 34
  Warfighting (FMFM-1, 1989), 36–37, 39–40
guerilla politics, 97
Guevara, Ernesto "Che," 97–98
Gulf War, 36–39
"Guns, God, and Gays" slogan, 17, 19–20, 26

harmony, initiative, variety, and rapidity, 43, 44, 45–46
Hayden, Tom, 94–97
Howard, John, 93
Human Factors on the Fireline (NWCG course L-180), 79
Hussein, Saddam, 36, 37, 39

IAF (Industrial Activities Foundation), 94
ICS (Incident Command System), 7, 75–79
ICTs (incident command teams), 83
Immigration Bill, 13
Inchon Landings, Korean War, 30
Incident Command for Single Resources or Initial Action Incidents (FEMA course IS-200), 75, 77–78, 81
Incident Command System (ICS), 7, 75–79
incident command teams (ICTs), 83
indirect approach, 64, 67
Industrial Activities Foundation (IAF), 94
infrastructure, social, 54
initiative, variety, rapidity, and harmony, 43, 44, 45–46
intelligence, 7, 34–35
Intelligence Preparation of the Battlefield (IPB)
  "Camp Casey" and, 91
  counter-recruitment and, 67
  definition of, 52
  event templating, 55–56
  flow chart, 101
  NAIs and DSTs, 56–57
  place of, 57–58
  understanding the battlefield, 52–54

understanding the threat or enemy, 54–55
Intermediate Nuclear Forces Treaty, 35–36
international peace and justice movement, 92–94, 97–98
Introduction to Incident Command System (FEMA course IS-100), 75, 77, 81
IPB. *See* Intelligence Preparation of the Battlefield
Iran, 4–5, 30
Iraq
antiwar movement and, 2–4
Gulf War, 36–39
war with Iran, 30
weapons inspections, 21–22
IS-100, Introduction to Incident Command System (FEMA course), 75, 77, 81
IS-200, Incident Command for Single Resources or Initial Action Incidents (FEMA course), 75, 77–78, 81

King, Martin Luther, 13–14
Korean War, 30

L-180, Human Factors on the Fireline (NWCG course), 79
L-280, From Followership to Leadership (NWCG course), 79
leadership
chain of command, 77–78
commander's intent, 32–33
development of leaders, 74–75, 80–82
followership and unity of command, 78–79, 82
Incident Command System (ICS), 7, 75–79
platoon leader's course (PLC), 29
strategy, operations, and tactics and, 62–63
Leading "Our" Way: Forward, Together, in the Progressive Movement (Williams, Makalani, and Parker), 17–19
learning to win, 89
lexicon, common, 77
Liddell Hart, B. H., 59, 64, 71
Lincoln, Abraham, 24
Lind, William, 31
Lombardi, Vince, 1
losing, 1–2

MacArthur, Douglas, 87
MAF (Marine Amphibious Force), 30
mainstream vs. progressive, 21
Makalani, Ahjamu, 17–19
maneuver warfare, 30–35, 36–37, 40
Marine Amphibious Force (MAF), 30
Marine Corps Air Ground Combat Center, 29
Marine Corps Combat Development Command, 30
Marine Corps Gazette, 30
Marshall, John, 25
Marxist-Leninist ideology, 93–94
mid-term elections (November 2006), 11, 21
mission objective, 32
motion, Newton's laws of, 48–49
Murtha, Jack, 3–4

Named Areas of Interest (NAIs), 56–57
Napoleon, 12, 13
National Concerned Citizens Activism Association (NCCAA) (proposed), 80–84
National Fire Protection Association (NFPA), 80
National Security Strategy (2006), 4–5
National Wildfire Coordination Group (NWCG), 79
NCCAA (National Concerned Citizens Activism Association) (proposed), 80–84
Nebenpunkt, 45
New Left, 94–97
Newton's laws of motion, 48–49
NFPA (National Fire Protection Association), 80

NWCG (National Wildfire Coordination Group), 79

observation, in OODA-Loop, 46. *See also* OODA-Loop
Obuszewski, Max, 11–12
On War (Clausewitz), 33
OODA-Loop (Observation-Orientation-Decision-Action time cycle), 103
  Boyd on, 42–43
  as broad-brush approach, 51–52
  execution of, 46–49
  ICS and, 76
  simulations and, 86
operations. *See* strategy, operations, and tactics
opponent. *See* enemy or opponent
organic synthesis collective (variety, rapidity, harmony, and initiative), 43, 44, 45–46
organizational structure. *See also* leadership
  antiwar movement's need for, 7–8
  "citizen participation" vs. "participatory democracy," 94–97
  flat-line model, 73–74, 95
  NCCAA (proposed), 80–84
  simulations or war gaming, 85–86
  standards, 80–82
organizational typing, 82–84
orientation, in OODA-Loop, 47. *See also* OODA-Loop
Orwell, George, 27

Parker, Brad, 17–19
participatory democracy, 94–97
patriotism, 25–26
Patterns of Conflict (Boyd), 42, 43
peace as objective, 15
performance benchmarks, 69
personnel support units (PSUs), 83
platoon leader's course (PLC), 29
politics, Clausewitz on, 44
pro-war movement
  as enemy to understand, 6–7
  simplicity in publicity campaigns of, 16–17
PSUs (personnel support units), 83
psychological and emotional factors in conflict, 45, 58

Rapid Deployment Force (RDF), 29–30
rapidity, harmony, initiative, and variety, 43, 44, 45–46
reaction vs. action, 49
recruitment and counter-recruitment, 63–68
religious right, 16–17, 20
Republican Guard, Iraqi, 37–39
Republican Party, 11
responsibilities, concept of, 77
revolutionary change, calls for, 96–97
Ritter, Scott
  family background, 28
  as intelligence officer, 29–30, 34–35
  in officer training, 28–29, 30–34
  as weapons inspector, 21–22, 35–36
Ritter Gets it Wrong: Why All the Negativity (Aumand and Breyman), 9–10
roles, concept of, 77

Schwarzkopf, Norman, 37, 39
Schwerpunkt, 45
Seattle, Washington, World Trade Organization demonstrations, 24
7th Marine Amphibious Brigade (MAG), 29–30
Sheehan, Cindy, 12–13, 14, 90, 91
simplicity and public appeal, 16–20
simulations, 85–86, 92
social infrastructure, 54
Soviet Union, 30, 35–36
span of control, 76
standards, 80–82
Steele, Michael, 37
strategy, operations, and tactics
  campaigning, art of, 69–71
  counter-recruitment example, 63–68
  definitions and distinctions, 60–61

  firefighting analogy, 61–62, 69
  lack of in antiwar movement, 5–6
  leadership and, 62–63
  logical continuum and linkages, 68–69
  OODA-Loop and, 48
  progressive movement's need for, 8–9, 59–60
Sun Tzu
  on *Chen* and *Chi* of combat, 43
  Clausewitz compared to, 45
  on ferocity, 88
  Gandhi vs., 14
  indirect approach and, 64
  on intelligence, 35
  Sheehan on, 12, 13
  on tactics without strategy, 60
supporters vs. allies, 92
survival, 1
systematic approach, 13–14

tactics. *See* strategy, operations, and tactics
TBS (The Basic School), 29
team structure, 83–84
templating, event, 55–56
The Basic School (TBS), 29
Thompson, Dorothy, xi
training programs
  FEMA, 75–77
  NWCG, 79
  platoon leader's course (PLC), 29
  for progressive movement, 79–82
transients, 42, 45
transportation support teams (TSTs), 84
Treichler, Rachel, 12
TSTs (transportation support teams), 84
Twenty-nine Palms, CA, 29–30, 34

United Nations Charter, 98, 127–61

values. *See* centers of gravity; core values
variety, rapidity, harmony, and initiative, 43, 44, 45–46
Vauvenargues, Luc de Clapiers de, 51
viability, 66
victory, 87–89
vision statements, 19–20, 25

war. *See also* Art of War
  American addiction to, 3
  art of campaigning, 69–71
  Clausewitz on, 44
  "fog" of, 44–45
  maneuver warfare, 30–35, 36–37, 40
Warfighting (Fleet Marine Force Manual, FMFM-1, 1989), 36–37, 39–40
war gaming, 85–86
weapons inspections, 21–22
"We the People," 25
Williams, Wayne, 17–19
winning, 87–89
World Trade Organization demonstrations (Seattle, 1999), 24
Wyly, Michael, 31

"Yin and Yang" philosophy of Sun Tzu, 33. *See also Art of War, The* (Sun Tzu); Sun Tzu